Teacher Edition

Level C

A Study Skills Curriculum

Zaner-Bloser

Reviewers:
Elizabeth Coates, Moss Side Middle School, Monroeville, Pennsylvania
Matthew A. Guyette, Lynnfield Middle School, Lynnfield, Massachusetts

Editorial Development: Kent Publishing Services

Design and Production: Signature Design Group

Cover Photos: *(top)* Globus, Holway & Lobel, The Stock Market; *(all others)* George C. Anderson

ISBN 0-7367-0004-8

Copyright © Zaner-Bloser, Inc.

All rights reserved. No part of this book may be reproduced or transmitted in any form or by any means, electronic or mechanical, including photocopying, recording, or by any information storage and retrieval system, without permission in writing from the Publisher.

Zaner-Bloser, Inc., P.O. Box 16764, Columbus, Ohio 43216-6764 (1-800-421-3018)

Printed in the United States of America

98 99 00 01 02 TPO 5 4 3 2 1

Table of Contents

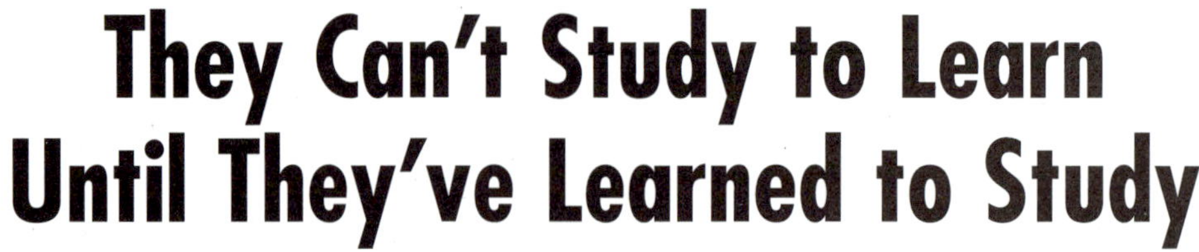

They Can't Study to Learn Until They've Learned to Study

You Can Take Charge! is a complete study skills program for middle school. Students learn the study and self-regulation skills that will help them become successful, productive learners in the classroom…and in life!

Level A
Gain Experience

Level B
Build Confidence

A study skills program that fits into the middle school curriculum

- Advisory period
- Homeroom period
- Language arts class
- Separate six- or nine-week study skills course
- After-school program
- Summer school
- Team teaching
- Content area teaching

All the skills your students need to study smarter and take charge of their own learning

- Managing time
- Organizing study space and materials
- Participating in class
- Using new strategies to boost comprehension
- Preparing speeches, reports, and projects
- Working effectively in groups
- Getting the most out of textbooks and references
- Improving test taking skills
- Coping with test anxiety
- Developing healthy habits that support learning

You Can Take Charge! is flexible, easy-to-teach, and designed to be used either throughout the year or as a mini-course in a variety of middle school settings. Zaner-Bloser's complete study skills program teaches students how to study—not just for tests, but for life. It helps build the foundation students need to succeed in middle school, high school, college, and beyond.

The *Take Charge!* Lesson

Self-Contained, Flexible, Engaging

Each ***Take Charge!*** lesson encourages collaboration and develops students' ability to work in a group. Students have many opportunities to evaluate their own study skills and attitudes, learn new strategies, and reflect on what works best for them.

Setting the Stage

Each lesson "hooks" the students with a short article that sets the stage and engages them in the topic. These brief topic introductions are a good opportunity to generate whole class discussion about the lesson's objectives.

Where Do You Stand?

Provides an opportunity for students to evaluate their own study habits and skills.

23 LESSON

Revising Notes

I hear and I forget.
I see and I remember.
I do and I understand.
—Chinese Proverb

Tell me and I'll forget.
Show me and I may not remember.
Involve me, and I'll understand.
—Native American Saying

Get Involved in Your Reading

One way to get involved in your reading is to read actively. And one way to read actively is to take notes. Deciding which notes to take makes you think about the ideas in your book. The act of writing them down helps you remember them.

Taking notes is the first step toward remembering what you read. Using your notes to remember what you read. Using your notes to study is another step. But what if you find that the notes you took quickly while you had the book in front of you are almost impossible to read when you need them? Don't worry. Revising your notes will bring everything back.

Where Do You Stand?

There are many good methods for revising notes. Some work better than others for different people, and some work best with different subjects. How many of these methods are familiar to you? Check the methods you are familiar with and the methods you use regularly.

Method	I know how to do this.	I use this method regularly.
Recopying		
Highlighting or color-coding		
Drawing webs		
Making outlines		
Organizing ideas on note cards		
Designing study sheets		

92 Level C • Achieve Mastery

Rate Yourself

If you're familiar with a variety of ways to revise notes, you're ahead of the game. If you regularly use different techniques, that's even better. It's a good idea to try different ways to revise notes. Then you can choose the methods that work best for you.

Sort It Out

In the next column, you'll find some notes taken by Kevin several weeks ago. With a little bit of revising, they'll be much more useful to Kevin. Read through the notes. Identify the main ideas and key details. Then organize and revise the notes in the space below by placing the information in a web or in an outline. If you really want to practice revising notes, make both a web and an outline!

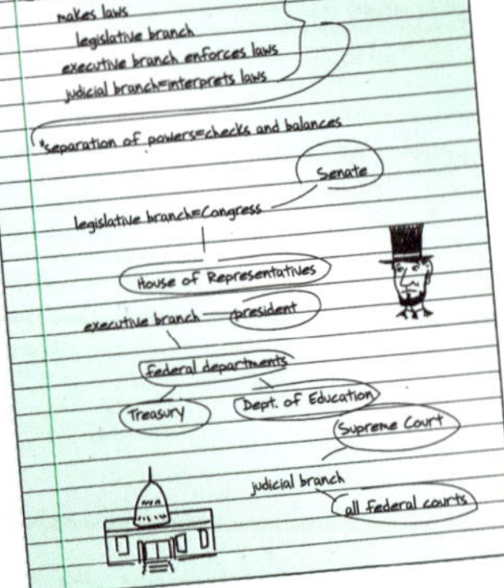

Unit 7 • Working With Textbooks and References 93

Focus Activities

Small group activities allow students to discuss the issue and puzzle out the learning for themselves.

Study Tips and Strategies

Lessons provide friendly advice, tips, and specific strategies to help students improve their study skills. There's something for everyone!

Methods for Revising Notes

Recopy Your Notes

Recopying your notes is an easy way to revise. When you recopy, you just rewrite your notes in your neatest handwriting, checking the spelling of key names and terms, and filling in any information that is unclear. When you recopy your notes, they are still organized in the same way, but they are easier to read and understand.

Recopying is easy, and it helps you remember. When you recopy, you have to look at your notes more carefully than you would if you just reread them. It also helps the information get to your brain through a different path—your sense of touch. If you read aloud as you recopy, you'll also be using your sense of hearing.

Highlight or Color Code

To make your recopied notes even more useful, you can go back and highlight, or color code, them. Make up a system that works well for the subject you're studying. In math, you might highlight formulas or definitions. For social studies, you might use one color for main ideas, another color for supporting details, and another color for names you want to remember. You can make your notes as colorful and creative as you please!

Design Graphic Organizers

You know that graphic organizers are good ways to organize information. If you think in pictures, using this method may help you see how ideas and facts are related. Plan your web ahead of time or just start writing ideas and see how it grows. The more personal you make your design, the easier it will be for you to remember the information. Here are two examples.

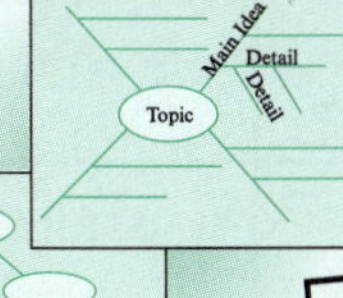

Topic
Main Idea
Detail

Make an Outline

An outline can make the organization of ideas very clear. It has a formal structure, with Roman numerals for main ideas and letters and numbers that show the relative importance of details. If you're an orderly person who likes everything to fit into just the right place, you may prefer making outlines to drawing maps or webs. Both methods help you organize information and show the relationships among ideas and details.

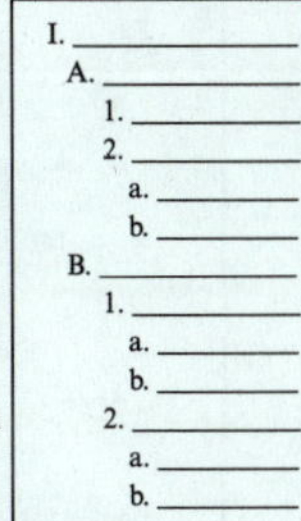

Organize With Note Cards

If you're a person who likes to work with your hands, using note cards to revise your notes may be just the thing for you. Once your notes have been copied onto the cards, you can move them around and use them in many ways. You can lay them out on your desk in the shape of a web. You can organize them like an outline. You can use them to quiz yourself to study for a test. And note cards are really portable. Put a rubber band around them and stick them in your pocket. Take them out to study while you're waiting in a long line or whenever you have a few minutes left at the end of a class.

Turn Your Notes Into Study Sheets

A study sheet is the final version of the raw notes that you have written and revised. It may include an outline, several graphic organizers, and complete paragraphs of information written in your own words. Once you've finalized your study sheets, put them all together in a three-ring binder. Use tabbed dividers to separate subjects.

When it's time for a test, you'll be able to use your study sheets to study better and faster. You'll know that you've got all the information you need in an organized, easy-to-read form. And once you feel organized, the rest is easy.

Take time to revise your "raw" notes into useful study aids.

Where Are You Going?

Summarize what you learned in this lesson. ____________________

Now use your summary to write a *Take Charge!* goal that will help you become a better student. ____________________

Where Are You Going?

Provides a space for students to summarize their own learning and to create a personal action plan.

Visit our Web site www.zaner-bloser.com

Take Charge! of Your Assignments

Week of ____________________

	Subject	Assignment	Due Date	Materials	✓➔
Monday					
Tuesday					
Wednesday					
Thursday					
Friday					

✓ = task complete

➔ = continue task next week

Copyright © Zaner-Bloser, Inc.
This page may be reproduced for classroom use.

Tips for Parents

Study Skills for Life

Helping your child develop good study habits can be a valuable gift from you to your child. While you may or may not actually work with your child as he or she does homework, you can set up an environment that will help your child be successful. You can also reinforce the instruction in ***You Can Take Charge!***, our study skills program, by following these suggestions.

- **Set aside a time to study.**
  With your child, decide on the best time to study each day. Then set that time aside every day, five days a week. If your child doesn't have homework one day, he or she can use that time to review for a test or to read ahead. Stick to the scheduled study time, every day. Late afternoon or early evening works best for many students, because it allows time to relax at the end of the day.

- **Plan for study breaks.**
  Short breaks will help your child study better. Schedule study breaks about every 20 minutes or after certain tasks are completed. A break of 5 or 10 minutes will help your child concentrate better on the rest of his or her work. Breaks shouldn't involve your child in something that will make it difficult to get back to work, like watching TV or talking on the phone.

- **Set aside a place to study.**
  Find a study spot that is free of distraction. A good place to study will have good lighting, a table or desk for written work, and a comfortable chair that encourages good posture and helps your child stay alert.

- **Keep study supplies handy.**
  Keeping homework supplies handy will save valuable study time. Basic supplies include paper, pencils, pen, eraser, ruler, colored markers or crayons, tape, paper clips, scissors, and a dictionary. Supplies can be kept in a drawer or in a box. Students also need a safe place to keep their class notes, homework, and quizzes so they'll be handy when it's time to review for a big test.

- **Eliminate distractions.**
  There are so many distractions! They may include other people talking or walking around, TV shows, the radio, electronic games, the telephone, and even a cluttered work area. Try to locate your child's study place away from distractions as much as possible. Some families try to make study time a quiet reading or work time for everyone in the family.

  Some students are able to study well with soft background music. The latest tunes are likely to be distracting, however, as students try to catch the lyrics. Recent studies show that classical music enhances the ability to concentrate in many people of all ages.

- **Avoid interruptions.**
  One hour of concentrated study is better than two hours full of interruptions. Ask your child to tell friends not to call or stop over during study time. Then take messages when these interruptions happen. Even chores shouldn't interrupt study time!

Copyright © Zaner-Bloser, Inc.
This page may be reproduced for classroom use.

Organizing Your Study Space

About Study Spaces

Some students need peace and quiet for studying, while others like background music. Some prefer to study alone, and others like to work with a friend. Some students study at home, while others study at an after-school center. All students need to evaluate their study habits to decide how and where they study best. In this lesson, students will learn how to find the study space that suits their personality. They will also learn that they can control and arrange their environment to create an organized and efficient study space. You may wish to distribute copies of the *Tips for Parents* (page 9 of this Teacher Edition) to the parents of your students.

Pages 4–5

- **A Space of Your Own**
  After students read the lesson introduction, invite volunteers to describe their favorite places to study.

- **Where Do You Stand?/Rate Yourself**
  Ask students to assess their study spaces by completing and evaluating the quiz on their own. As students discuss the results, model good organizational skills by sharing some strategies you use to organize your work space (see *Teacher Modeling*).

- **Be a Designer**
  Students will form a concrete picture of their ideal study space as they design their floor plan. Stress that since the space is an ideal, students can include anything they want. If you prefer, ask students to list items to include instead of drawing them.

- **Spruce Up Your Study Space**
  This is the time for students to get practical. Invite groups to explain why they chose certain study space features as the most important. Then encourage students to work on their own to think of an imaginative way to incorporate one idea into their study space right away.

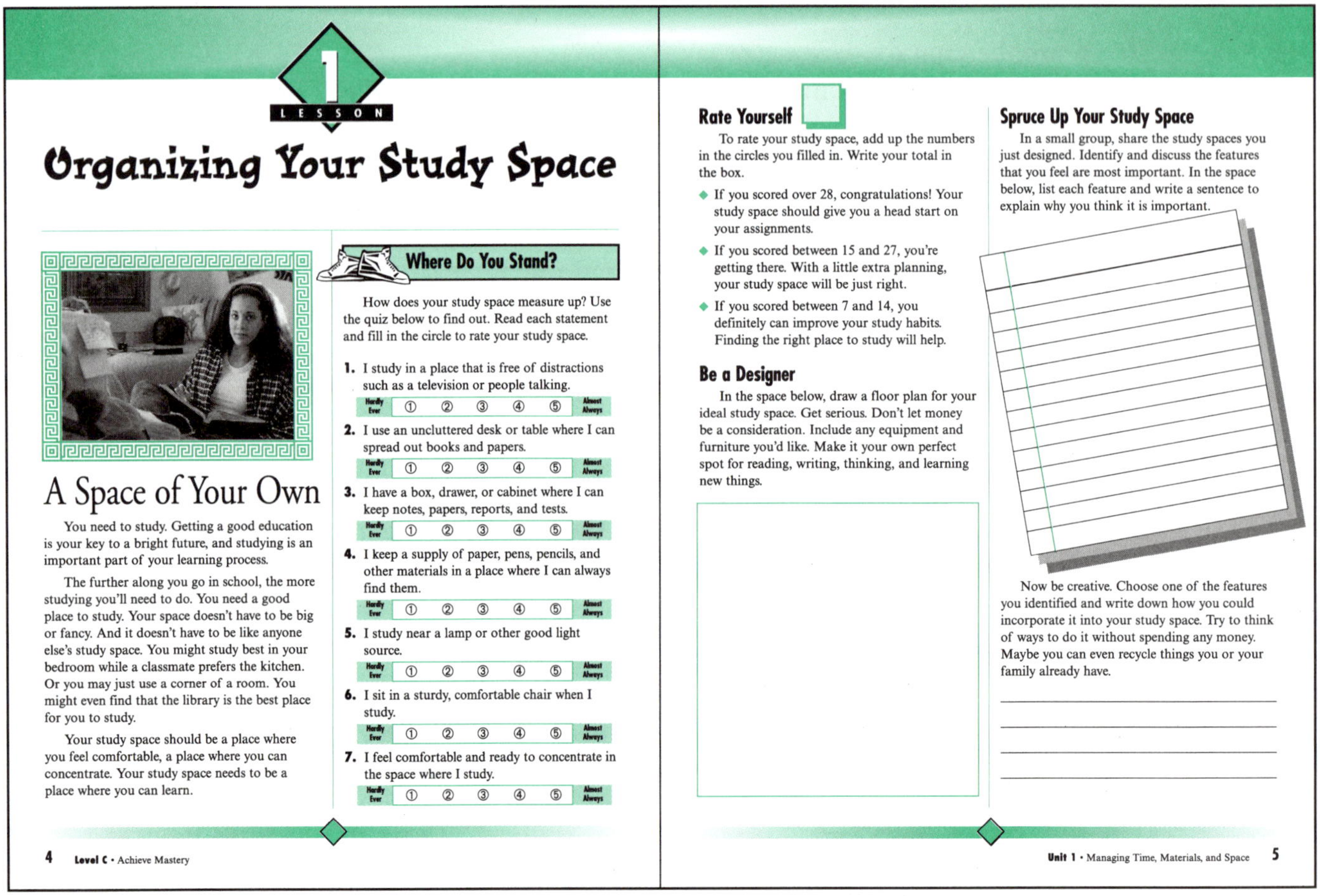

1 LESSON

Organizing Your Study Space

A Space of Your Own

You need to study. Getting a good education is your key to a bright future, and studying is an important part of your learning process.

The further along you go in school, the more studying you'll need to do. You need a good place to study. Your space doesn't have to be big or fancy. And it doesn't have to be like anyone else's study space. You might study best in your bedroom while a classmate prefers the kitchen. Or you may just use a corner of a room. You might even find that the library is the best place for you to study.

Your study space should be a place where you feel comfortable, a place where you can concentrate. Your study space needs to be a place where you can learn.

Where Do You Stand?

How does your study space measure up? Use the quiz below to find out. Read each statement and fill in the circle to rate your study space.

1. I study in a place that is free of distractions such as a television or people talking.
   Hardly Ever ① ② ③ ④ ⑤ Almost Always
2. I use an uncluttered desk or table where I can spread out books and papers.
   Hardly Ever ① ② ③ ④ ⑤ Almost Always
3. I have a box, drawer, or cabinet where I can keep notes, papers, reports, and tests.
   Hardly Ever ① ② ③ ④ ⑤ Almost Always
4. I keep a supply of paper, pens, pencils, and other materials in a place where I can always find them.
   Hardly Ever ① ② ③ ④ ⑤ Almost Always
5. I study near a lamp or other good light source.
   Hardly Ever ① ② ③ ④ ⑤ Almost Always
6. I sit in a sturdy, comfortable chair when I study.
   Hardly Ever ① ② ③ ④ ⑤ Almost Always
7. I feel comfortable and ready to concentrate in the space where I study.
   Hardly Ever ① ② ③ ④ ⑤ Almost Always

4 Level C • Achieve Mastery

Rate Yourself

To rate your study space, add up the numbers in the circles you filled in. Write your total in the box.

- If you scored over 28, congratulations! Your study space should give you a head start on your assignments.
- If you scored between 15 and 27, you're getting there. With a little extra planning, your study space will be just right.
- If you scored between 7 and 14, you definitely can improve your study habits. Finding the right place to study will help.

Be a Designer

In the space below, draw a floor plan for your ideal study space. Get serious. Don't let money be a consideration. Include any equipment and furniture you'd like. Make it your own perfect spot for reading, writing, thinking, and learning new things.

Spruce Up Your Study Space

In a small group, share the study spaces you just designed. Identify and discuss the features that you feel are most important. In the space below, list each feature and write a sentence to explain why you think it is important.

Now be creative. Choose one of the features you identified and write down how you could incorporate it into your study space. Try to think of ways to do it without spending any money. Maybe you can even recycle things you or your family already have.

Unit 1 • Managing Time, Materials, and Space 5

Pages 6–7

- **Knickknacks or Not? Organizing Your Materials**
  Take a poll to see how students feel about decorations in their study space. Then focus students' attention on essentials by asking them to categorize study materials. Remind them to list basic supplies such as pens, paper, and notebooks. Suggest they use their lists as checklists to help them organize materials.
- **Make Your Study Space Grow**
  Emphasize that plants are beneficial to the atmosphere. Encourage students to put a plant in their study space to see what happens.
- **Read It Right**
  Changing the position of a book is a no-cost strategy students can use right away. Suggest that students try it and report the results.
- **Where Are You Going?**
  Ask students to write a goal that tells how they plan to improve their own study area.

Teacher Modeling

You may wish to use or adapt these examples of teacher modeling.

To organize my work space:

- I keep the top of my desk uncluttered so I always have room to write.
- I keep pens, paper clips, scissors, tape, and other supplies I use often in a desk organizer.
- I have an "In" basket on my desk.
- I keep a notebook with my daily teaching plans right beside me at all times.
- I organize my papers by subject in a filing cabinet.
- I clean up materials I used for one project before beginning my next task.
- I sit beside a good lamp when I read or grade papers.
- I hold my work materials in a comfortable position so I won't tire quickly.

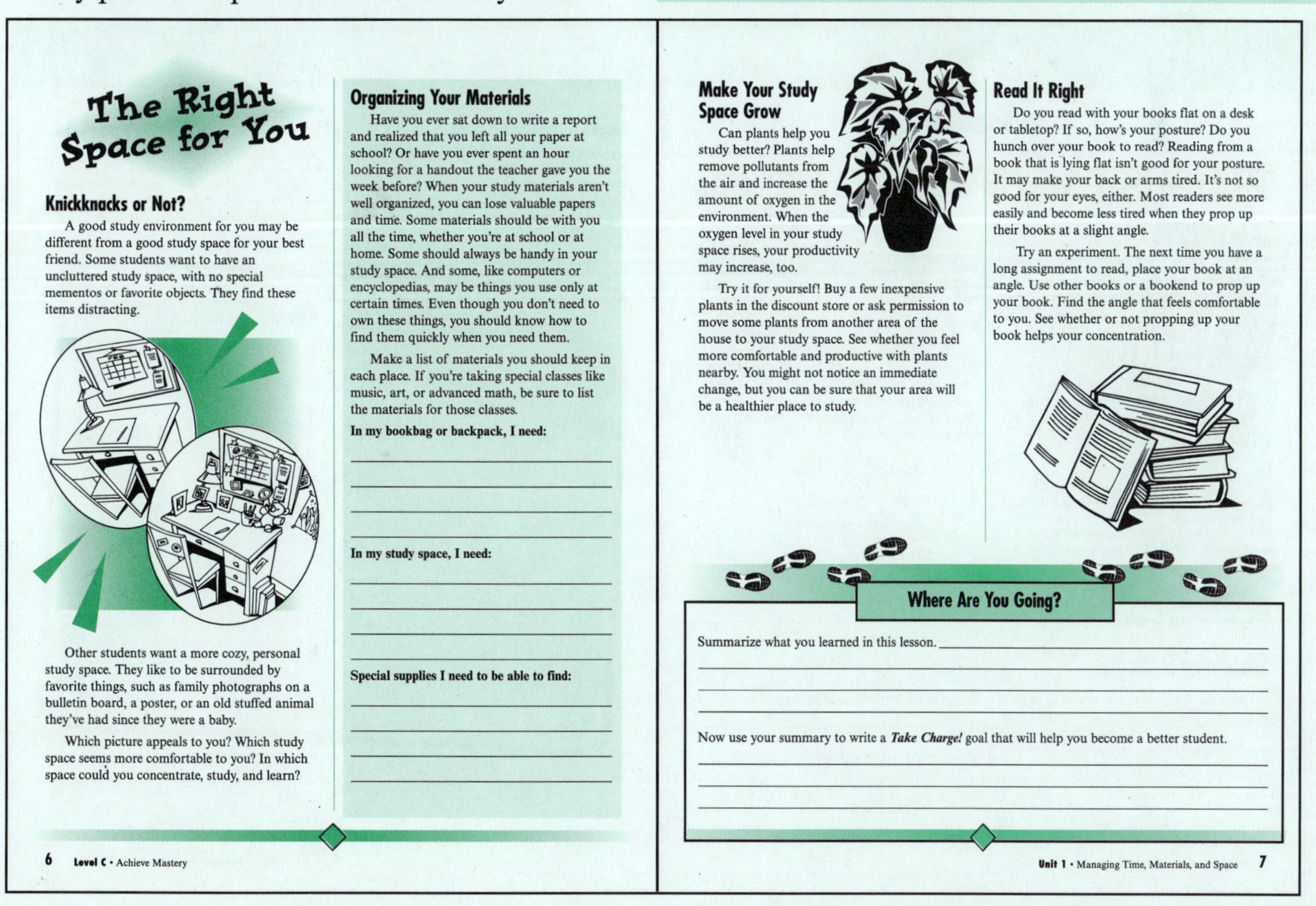

The Right Space for You

Knickknacks or Not?

A good study environment for you may be different from a good study space for your best friend. Some students want to have an uncluttered study space, with no special mementos or favorite objects. They find these items distracting.

Other students want a more cozy, personal study space. They like to be surrounded by favorite things, such as family photographs on a bulletin board, a poster, or an old stuffed animal they've had since they were a baby.

Which picture appeals to you? Which study space seems more comfortable to you? In which space could you concentrate, study, and learn?

Organizing Your Materials

Have you ever sat down to write a report and realized that you left all your paper at school? Or have you ever spent an hour looking for a handout the teacher gave you the week before? When your study materials aren't well organized, you can lose valuable papers and time. Some materials should be with you all the time, whether you're at school or at home. Some should always be handy in your study space. And some, like computers or encyclopedias, may be things you use only at certain times. Even though you don't need to own these things, you should know how to find them quickly when you need them.

Make a list of materials you should keep in each place. If you're taking special classes like music, art, or advanced math, be sure to list the materials for those classes.

In my bookbag or backpack, I need:

In my study space, I need:

Special supplies I need to be able to find:

6 **Level C** • Achieve Mastery

Make Your Study Space Grow

Can plants help you study better? Plants help remove pollutants from the air and increase the amount of oxygen in the environment. When the oxygen level in your study space rises, your productivity may increase, too.

Try it for yourself! Buy a few inexpensive plants in the discount store or ask permission to move some plants from another area of the house to your study space. See whether you feel more comfortable and productive with plants nearby. You might not notice an immediate change, but you can be sure that your area will be a healthier place to study.

Read It Right

Do you read with your books flat on a desk or tabletop? If so, how's your posture? Do you hunch over your book to read? Reading from a book that is lying flat isn't good for your posture. It may make your back or arms tired. It's not so good for your eyes, either. Most readers see more easily and become less tired when they prop up their books at a slight angle.

Try an experiment. The next time you have a long assignment to read, place your book at an angle. Use other books or a bookend to prop up your book. Find the angle that feels comfortable to you. See whether or not propping up your book helps your concentration.

Where Are You Going?

Summarize what you learned in this lesson. ____________

Now use your summary to write a ***Take Charge!*** goal that will help you become a better student.

Unit 1 • Managing Time, Materials, and Space 7

Planning Work and Free Time

About Planning

Do your students often complain that they never have enough time for all the things they want to do? Classes, homework, after-school activities, friends, and family all compete for their time. It's important for students to realize that with good planning they can get their work done and have time for fun, too. Managing time well is a key to being productive, both in and out of school. In this lesson, students will learn to accept responsibility for scheduling homework time and free time. As they get used to planning ahead, students may find that they have more free time than ever before.

Pages 8–9

- **Scheduling Strategies**
  Where Do You Stand?
  Invite volunteers to read aloud Anna's and Steve's scheduling strategies. Then encourage students to fill out the activities inventory as a way to daydream about what they would do if they had extra time. Ask students to explain their own strategies for scheduling homework and other activities. Share some strategies you use to schedule work and free time (see *Teacher Modeling*).

- **Make a Weekly Schedule**
  To introduce the activity, share your own daily or weekly schedule with students. Then ask them to complete the planner on their own. Remind students to include blocks of time for studying, after-school activities, homework, dinner, and relaxing. Discuss realistic time estimates for particular activities. Suggest that if students are not sure how long an activity will take, they should plan more time than they expect to need, not less. Students can compare their schedules with a partner to look for conflicts or for activities they left out. Invite volunteers to share how they found time for the new activity they plan to try.

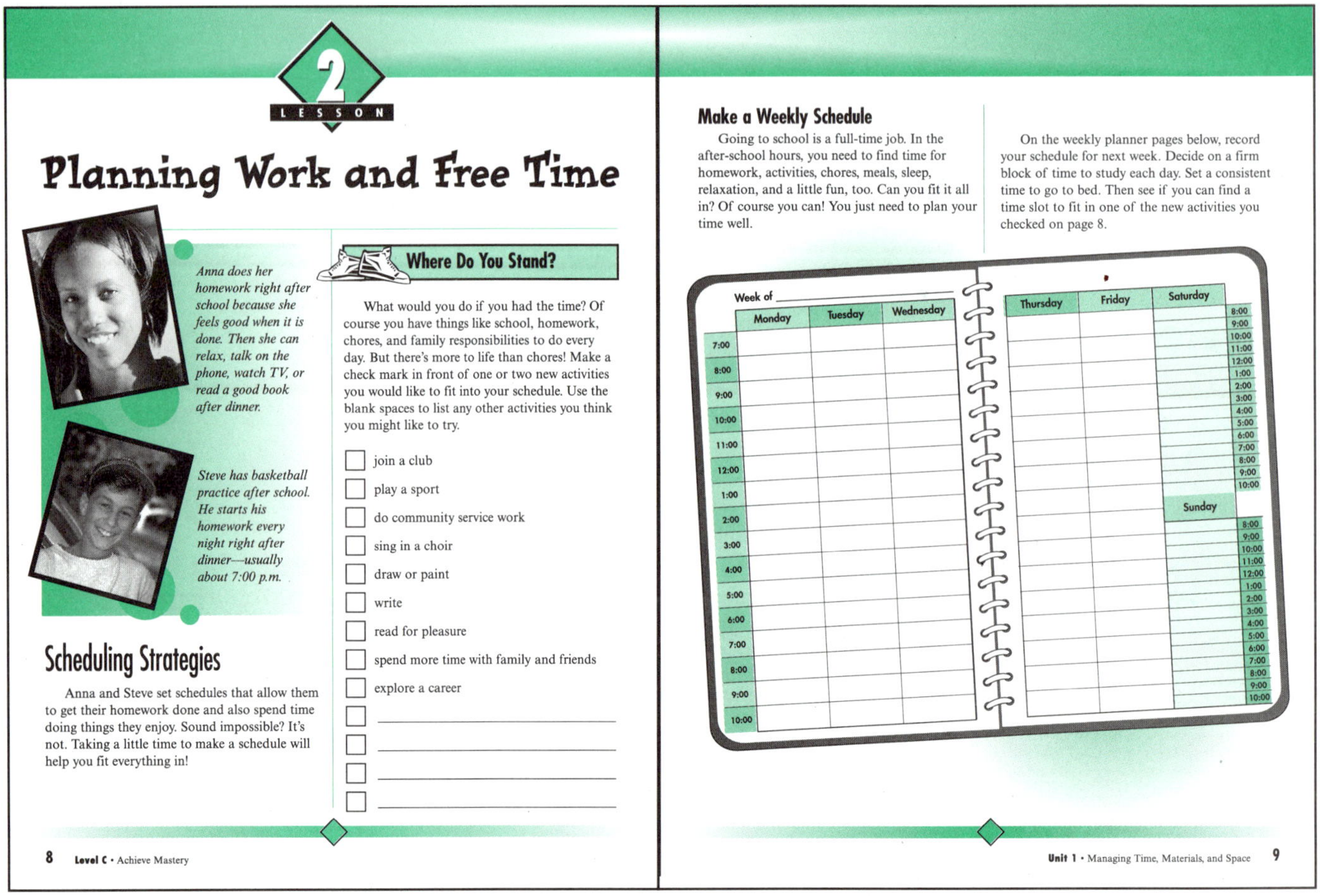

2 LESSON

Planning Work and Free Time

Anna does her homework right after school because she feels good when it is done. Then she can relax, talk on the phone, watch TV, or read a good book after dinner.

Steve has basketball practice after school. He starts his homework every night right after dinner—usually about 7:00 p.m.

Scheduling Strategies

Anna and Steve set schedules that allow them to get their homework done and also spend time doing things they enjoy. Sound impossible? It's not. Taking a little time to make a schedule will help you fit everything in!

Where Do You Stand?

What would you do if you had the time? Of course you have things like school, homework, chores, and family responsibilities to do every day. But there's more to life than chores! Make a check mark in front of one or two new activities you would like to fit into your schedule. Use the blank spaces to list any other activities you think you might like to try.

- ☐ join a club
- ☐ play a sport
- ☐ do community service work
- ☐ sing in a choir
- ☐ draw or paint
- ☐ write
- ☐ read for pleasure
- ☐ spend more time with family and friends
- ☐ explore a career
- ☐ ____________
- ☐ ____________
- ☐ ____________
- ☐ ____________

8 **Level C** • Achieve Mastery

Make a Weekly Schedule

Going to school is a full-time job. In the after-school hours, you need to find time for homework, activities, chores, meals, sleep, relaxation, and a little fun, too. Can you fit it all in? Of course you can! You just need to plan your time well.

On the weekly planner pages below, record your schedule for next week. Decide on a firm block of time to study each day. Set a consistent time to go to bed. Then see if you can find a time slot to fit in one of the new activities you checked on page 8.

Week of ____________

	Monday	Tuesday	Wednesday
7:00			
8:00			
9:00			
10:00			
11:00			
12:00			
1:00			
2:00			
3:00			
4:00			
5:00			
6:00			
7:00			
8:00			
9:00			
10:00			

Thursday	Friday

Saturday	
8:00	
9:00	
10:00	
11:00	
12:00	
1:00	
2:00	
3:00	
4:00	
5:00	
6:00	
7:00	
8:00	
9:00	
10:00	

Sunday	
8:00	
9:00	
10:00	
11:00	
12:00	
1:00	
2:00	
3:00	
4:00	
5:00	
6:00	
7:00	
8:00	
9:00	
10:00	

Unit 1 • Managing Time, Materials, and Space 9

Pages 10–11

- **Start a "To-Do" List**
  Prioritize Your List
  After students read these sections, ask them to keep and prioritize a daily to-do list for a week. Stress that the lists should include homework assignments, chores, after-school activities, and plans with friends. If your students don't have their own assignment notebooks, you may wish to copy and distribute the generic weekly planner on page 8 of this Teacher Edition.
- **Scheduling Tips**
  Ask students to read these tips for refining their scheduling techniques. Invite volunteers to tell which tip they think is hardest to follow and which one they find most useful.
- **Where Are You Going?**
  Ask students to write a goal that includes at least one change they plan to make in the way they schedule work and free time.

Teacher Modeling

You may wish to use or adapt these examples of teacher modeling.

To plan ahead:

- I make a weekly schedule that includes appointments, meetings, and activities.
- At the end of every day, I make a to-do list for the next day. Then I prioritize my list to decide which tasks are most important.
- I check off items on my list as I complete them to feel a sense of accomplishment.

To balance work and free time:

- I schedule work first. Then I can enjoy free time as a reward for completing my work.
- I try to overestimate the amount of time it will take me to complete my work instead of underestimating.
- I keep my eye on the clock to make sure I stick to my schedule.

Tips for Scheduling Your Time

Start a "To-Do" List

A weekly schedule is a good thing to have, but you may find that it's too general to keep you on track every day. To make sure you're completing all the tasks you need to accomplish each day, you may want to make a daily to-do list.

Your daily to-do list includes all the tasks you need to do each day to keep yourself on schedule. It may include homework assignments, chores, after-school activities, and plans with friends. Check your to-do list every morning. Each night before you go to bed, check your to-do list again. Cross off every task you've completed. Then make a new to-do list for the next day. Put any tasks you didn't complete on tomorrow's list.

TO DO
Feed the cat
Study for test
Go to practice
Do math homework
Take out the trash
Read next chapter for English
Call for concert tickets

If you find that you hardly ever accomplish everything on your list, you may be underestimating the time you need for each task. Take a hard look at your schedule. Are you forgetting to schedule travel time or time for snacks and breaks? Do you need to allow more time for your homework? You may need to revise your schedule.

Prioritize Your List

You have many different jobs to do every day. Some are more important than others. Some tasks, like studying for tests, lead to important life goals. Others, like feeding your fish, are so easy to do that they seem trivial, but they are important, too. Some need to be done, but they don't need to be completed right away. Other jobs on your list really don't matter very much at all. It won't hurt to put them off until tomorrow. In fact, it may not matter if you never get around to them at all.

The problem is that those less important activities are often easier and more enjoyable than the important ones. It's tempting to do the easy job instead of the harder but more important one. What would you rather do—start a big science project or arrange your CD collection?

Sometimes it's hard to make the right choice. Just remember, you need to make sure the important things get done. Take a good hard look at your list and prioritize your work. Decide which tasks are important. Then make sure you get them done.

To prioritize your to-do list, decide which of your obligations are most urgent. Write a number *1* in front of these jobs. Then decide which things are least urgent. Give these a number *3*. Finally, place a number *2* next to the other tasks that come between—the things that have to get done but not right now. Then work through the jobs on your list, starting with the most urgent. Cross off each job as you complete it.

1 2 3

10 **Level C** • Achieve Mastery

Scheduling Tips

- **Set realistic goals.** Giving yourself two hours to complete a four-hour job just sets you up for failure.
- **Avoid marathon study sessions.** Working on science for an hour a day for a week is usually easier and more productive than doing six hours of science on Sunday evening. When you schedule a study marathon for yourself, you're likely to find that it's hard to stay focused and efficient.
- **Allow time for chores and errands.** Don't forget to schedule everyday tasks such as doing dishes or walking your dog.
- **Schedule time for fun.** It's important to have fun. After you've let yourself "waste" a little time, you'll find that it's easier to settle down to work.
- **Plan a regular time for study.** When you study at the same time every day, studying will become part of your daily routine. You'll find it easier to get started and to stay focused.
- **Stick to your schedule.** Once you've started to work, don't let any distractions interrupt your study time.
- **Reward yourself.** Schedule a reward, like playing a video game, watching television, or calling a friend, after each difficult task. Your reward will give you an incentive to keep going.
- **Take time to plan.** Schedule ten minutes each evening to plan your time for the next day. When morning comes, you'll be all ready to go.

School is a full-time job. But you can get your schoolwork done and still have time left over to do things you enjoy by trying some of these tips.

Where Are You Going?

Summarize what you learned in this lesson. ____________________

Now use your summary to write a *Take Charge!* goal that will help you become a better student.

____

Unit 1 • Managing Time, Materials, and Space 11

Setting Goals

About Goals

This lesson shows students how to set long-term, short-term, and daily goals. Setting goals helps students stay focused and motivated to learn. Once students develop the habit of setting goals, they will discover that their studying has direction and that they are motivated to set and reach more and more difficult goals.

Pages 12–13

◆ **Getting There**
After students read the lesson introduction, invite them to discuss the Chinese proverb. Ask them to tell how setting a goal is like taking the first step of a long journey.

◆ **Where Do You Stand?/Rate Yourself**
Ask students to assess and evaluate the techniques they already use to set and meet goals by completing and evaluating the quiz.

◆ **Long-Term Goals**
Talk About It
If students have difficulty brainstorming a list of life goals, suggest that they read *Talk About It* first. Picturing themselves as adults will help students think of accomplishments they would be proud to tell their friends about in the future. Guide them in writing specific, clear, and measurable goals. Students can share their goals by acting out the reunion in small groups.

◆ **Short-Term Goals**
Daily Goals
After students complete their lists, suggest that they go back and explain how accomplishing each short-term goal leads to achieving a long-term goal. Encourage discussion about how setting daily goals helps students meet short-term goals. Some students may enjoy making flowcharts to show how each accomplishment leads to the next.

3
LESSON

Setting Goals

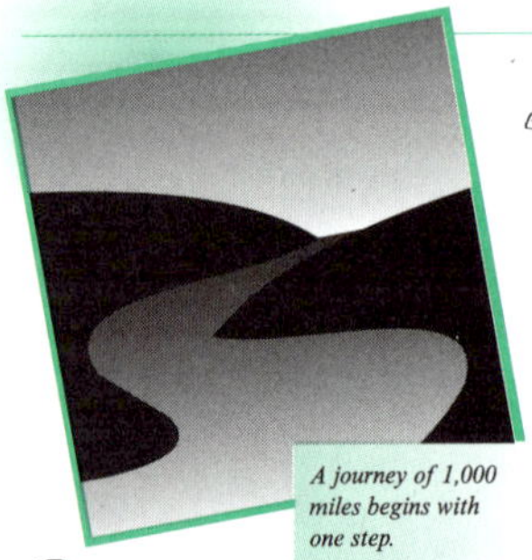

A journey of 1,000 miles begins with one step.
—Chinese Proverb

GETTING THERE

When you set off on a trip, you usually know where you're going. You know where your journey begins, and a map shows just how to get to your destination. Working to accomplish a life goal is a different kind of journey. Unfortunately, the path to accomplishing a life goal like going to college or having a career isn't always clear. You need to set a goal and stick to it, no matter what. One thing's for sure. You'll never get there until you take that first step. And that first step is setting your goal.

Where Do You Stand?

How good are you at setting goals? Check each statement that is usually true for you.

- ☐ I regularly plan and schedule my time.
- ☐ I make daily to-do lists.
- ☐ I seldom feel behind in my work.
- ☐ I finish projects in a timely fashion.
- ☐ I rarely have to give excuses for not getting things done.
- ☐ I have clear, specific daily goals I want to accomplish.
- ☐ I have short-term goals for things I want to accomplish this year.
- ☐ I have long-term goals for becoming the person I want to be, and I make choices to help me achieve them.

Rate Yourself

- ◆ If you checked all eight statements, congratulations! You have excellent goal-setting habits.
- ◆ If you checked between three and seven of the statements, you can use some practice with setting realistic goals.
- ◆ If you checked only one or two statements, you'll find that setting goals will help you make the most of your time.

12 **Level C** • Achieve Mastery

Long-Term Goals

Long-term goals are goals you set now and achieve in the future. Long-term goals may take five, fifteen, or even twenty-five years to achieve. To set a long-term goal, imagine what you want your life to be like in the future. Where will you be? Who will you become?

Brainstorm a list of your long-term goals and write them on the lines. Don't worry, long-term plans aren't set in stone; they will change as you learn more about yourself and the world.

Talk About It

Now get together with a small group of classmates. Pretend that you're attending a middle school reunion twenty years from now. Imagine that you're sitting around a dinner table. Tell what you've accomplished in the years since you last saw each other.

January 2020

Short-Term Goals

Short-term goals are goals you can accomplish in a few months or a year. Brainstorm a list of things you would like to accomplish before the beginning of the next school year. Include steps that lead toward your long-term goals, as well as activities you find satisfying and enjoyable.

Daily Goals

Daily goals tell you exactly what you can do today to move your life ahead in the right direction. Most daily goals are small steps toward short-term goals. Lists of daily goals are also called to-do lists. Remember, as you complete things on your to-do list, cross them off. At the end of each day, make a new to-do list for the next day.

Make a to-do list for tomorrow on the lines below.

Unit 1 • Managing Time, Materials, and Space 13

Pages 14–15

- **Chart Your Course (Near and Far)**
  After reading the advice about setting goals, ask students to discuss how to set goals that are realistic, but not too easy to reach. Discuss how posting goal statements in plain sight can keep students on track. Remind students that their long-term goals are likely to change many times throughout their lives.
- **Tips for Goal-Setting**
  Ask volunteers to read the tips aloud. Then invite students to share their own goal-setting tips. Share strategies you use to set different kinds of goals (see *Teacher Modeling*).
- **Sample Goals**
  After reading this section, suggest that students review and revise the goals they wrote on page 13.
- **Where Are You Going?**
  Ask students to write a planning goal that will help them establish and accomplish life goals.

Teacher Modeling

You may wish to use or adapt these examples of teacher modeling.

To set goals:

- I establish goals that are realistic and achievable.
- I set specific short-term goals and reward myself when I accomplish them.
- I write my long-term goals on an index card. I keep the card taped to my bathroom mirror, where I see it every day.
- I limit my number of goals, so I can stay focused and accomplish them.
- If I feel impatient about the time it takes to achieve a long-term goal, I concentrate on the many short-term goals I've accomplished.

Chart Your Course (Near and Far)

Tips for Goal-Setting

- Make your goals clear, specific, and measurable. For example, *I will complete and turn in every homework assignment in social studies* is clearer than *I will do better in social studies.*
- Be sure your goals are realistic and achievable. Set goals that are within your reach.
- Phrase your goals positively. For example, *I will pass all my math quizzes* is much more encouraging than *I'm not going to get any Fs.*
- Set a reasonable number of goals. If you make too many goals, you may be so confused you won't accomplish any of them.
- Think of achieving your goals as a game and a challenge rather than a chore.
- Team up with a friend. Cheer for each other whenever one of you accomplishes a goal. Encourage each other when reaching a goal seems too hard.
- Be patient. Don't expect to meet your goals immediately. It takes time to learn new habits.
- Have confidence in yourself. Having a positive attitude will help you reach your goals.
- Don't be afraid to adjust your goals. Everyone changes as they grow. Sometimes goals change, too.

Motivate Yourself

Whenever you sit down to set goals, keep in mind your reasons for making them. Goals can keep you focused. If you understand that it's necessary to study math now to get into college later, you'll feel better about finishing those math problems each night. Goals are your motivation, or driving force, for being in school, studying, and learning.

Reach for the Stars

When you were a young child, you may have planned to be a professional athlete or a movie star. By now you probably realize that very few people reach those peaks. Some careers require special talents that people are born with. Be realistic, but don't let your realistic attitude keep you from aiming high. And don't be afraid to try hard things or things that take a long time. If you set goals that are too easy to reach, you may be disappointed later.

Keep Track of Your Goals

Write your long- and short-term goals on note cards. Post your goals in places where you will see them often, such as in your school locker, on your bulletin board, or on your bathroom mirror. Your written goals will be constant and motivating reminders of what you're trying to achieve.

14 Level C • Achieve Mastery

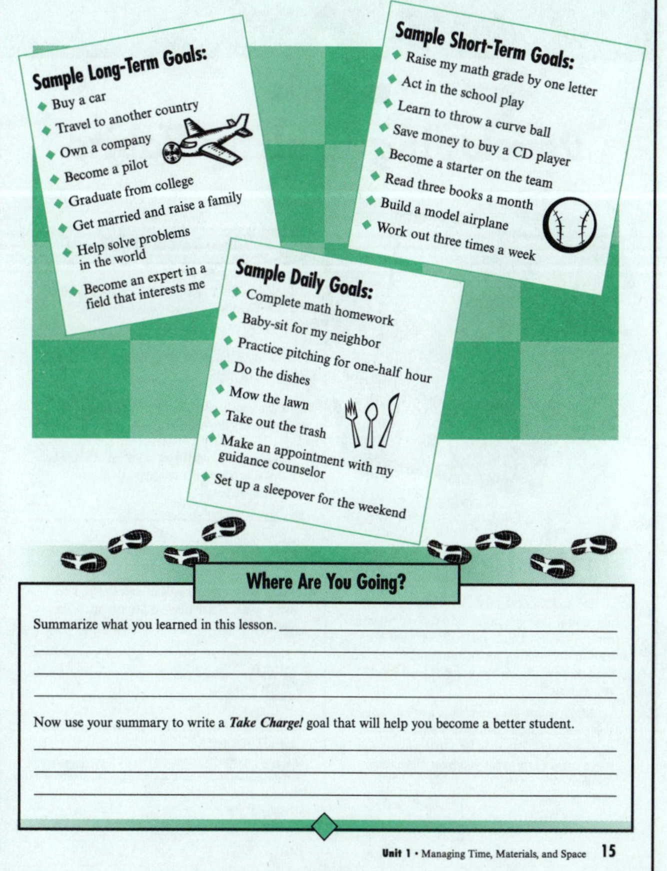

Sample Long-Term Goals:
- Buy a car
- Travel to another country
- Own a company
- Become a pilot
- Graduate from college
- Get married and raise a family
- Help solve problems in the world
- Become an expert in a field that interests me

Sample Short-Term Goals:
- Raise my math grade by one letter
- Act in the school play
- Learn to throw a curve ball
- Save money to buy a CD player
- Become a starter on the team
- Read three books a month
- Build a model airplane
- Work out three times a week

Sample Daily Goals:
- Complete math homework
- Baby-sit for my neighbor
- Practice pitching for one-half hour
- Do the dishes
- Mow the lawn
- Take out the trash
- Make an appointment with my guidance counselor
- Set up a sleepover for the weekend

Where Are You Going?

Summarize what you learned in this lesson. ______________________

Now use your summary to write a *Take Charge!* goal that will help you become a better student. ______________________

Unit 1 • Managing Time, Materials, and Space 15

Developing Healthy Habits

About Healthy Habits

To succeed in school, students need to get plenty of sleep, eat well-balanced meals, and exercise frequently. But students often forget to make healthy habits a part of their daily routine. The purpose of this lesson is to help students understand that they can easily incorporate healthy habits into their everyday lives. A healthy lifestyle will help students feel better, increase their energy, be more productive, and improve their concentration.

Pages 16–17

◆ **To Your Health**
After students read the introduction, ask volunteers to describe healthy habits they already practice. Discuss the benefits of activities such as taking a daily walk, getting plenty of sleep, and choosing fruits and vegetables instead of candy for a snack.

◆ **Where Do You Stand?/Rate Yourself**
Encourage students to answer as honestly as possible to get a true picture of their current health habits. Emphasize that students will not be required to share their inventory answers.

◆ **Take a Sleep Survey**
After students complete their surveys and calculate the average amount of sleep for both survey populations, invite groups to compare their results and draw conclusions about them. Extend the activity by asking small groups to design posters that encourage their classmates to get a good night's sleep.

◆ **Plan for Healthy Eating**
Students can complete their food favorites list independently. Most will find that there are some foods they like in every category. Make sure they understand that the lower categories on the pyramid are the healthiest choices.

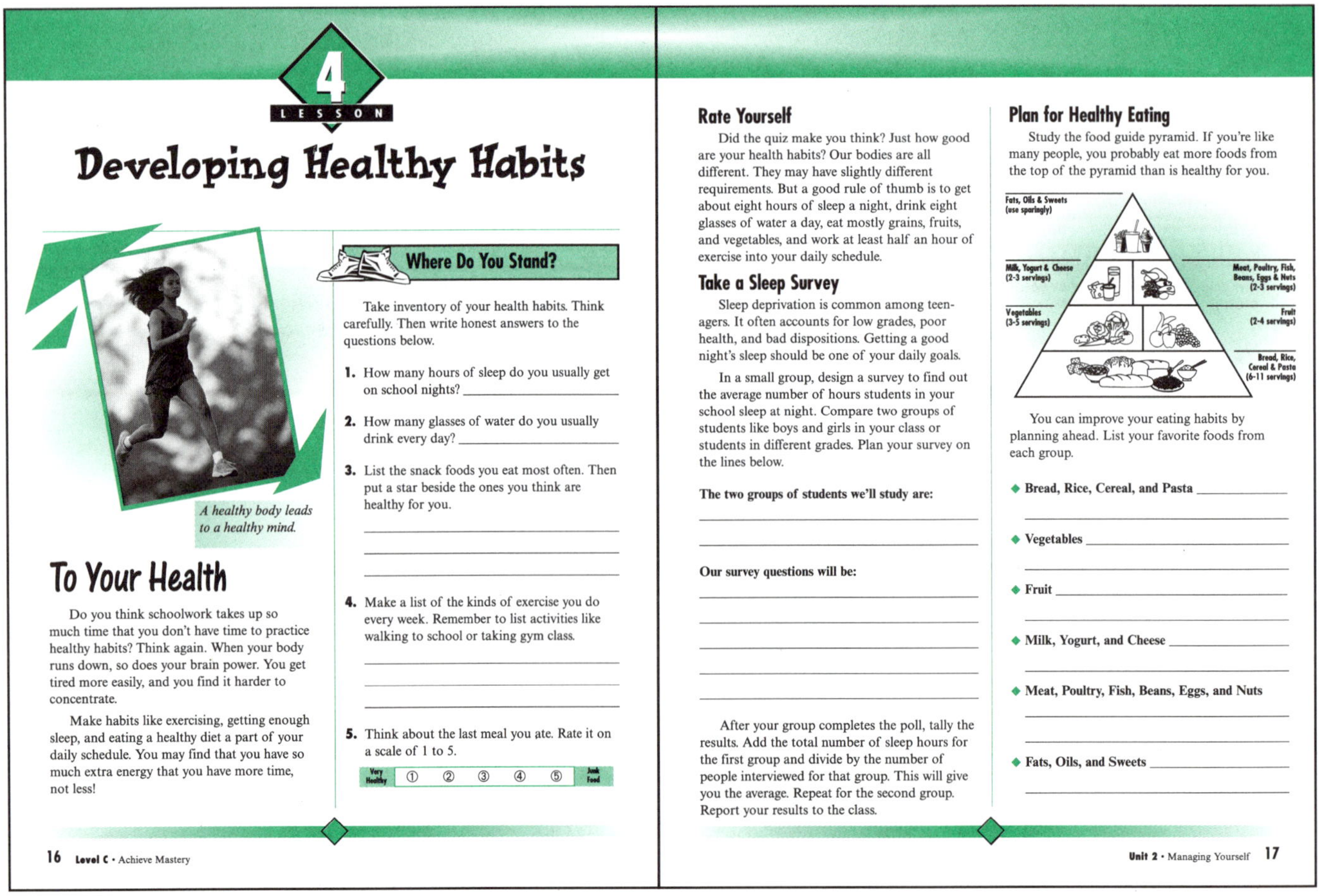

---

4 LESSON

Developing Healthy Habits

A healthy body leads to a healthy mind.

To Your Health

Do you think schoolwork takes up so much time that you don't have time to practice healthy habits? Think again. When your body runs down, so does your brain power. You get tired more easily, and you find it harder to concentrate.

Make habits like exercising, getting enough sleep, and eating a healthy diet a part of your daily schedule. You may find that you have so much extra energy that you have more time, not less!

Where Do You Stand?

Take inventory of your health habits. Think carefully. Then write honest answers to the questions below.

1. How many hours of sleep do you usually get on school nights? ____________
2. How many glasses of water do you usually drink every day? ____________
3. List the snack foods you eat most often. Then put a star beside the ones you think are healthy for you.
4. Make a list of the kinds of exercise you do every week. Remember to list activities like walking to school or taking gym class.
5. Think about the last meal you ate. Rate it on a scale of 1 to 5.

Very Healthy ① ② ③ ④ ⑤ Junk Food

16 Level C • Achieve Mastery

Rate Yourself

Did the quiz make you think? Just how good are your health habits? Our bodies are all different. They may have slightly different requirements. But a good rule of thumb is to get about eight hours of sleep a night, drink eight glasses of water a day, eat mostly grains, fruits, and vegetables, and work at least half an hour of exercise into your daily schedule.

Take a Sleep Survey

Sleep deprivation is common among teenagers. It often accounts for low grades, poor health, and bad dispositions. Getting a good night's sleep should be one of your daily goals.

In a small group, design a survey to find out the average number of hours students in your school sleep at night. Compare two groups of students like boys and girls in your class or students in different grades. Plan your survey on the lines below.

The two groups of students we'll study are:

Our survey questions will be:

After your group completes the poll, tally the results. Add the total number of sleep hours for the first group and divide by the number of people interviewed for that group. This will give you the average. Repeat for the second group. Report your results to the class.

Plan for Healthy Eating

Study the food guide pyramid. If you're like many people, you probably eat more foods from the top of the pyramid than is healthy for you.

Fats, Oils & Sweets (use sparingly)
Milk, Yogurt & Cheese (2-3 servings)
Meat, Poultry, Fish, Beans, Eggs & Nuts (2-3 servings)
Vegetables (3-5 servings)
Fruit (2-4 servings)
Bread, Rice, Cereal & Pasta (6-11 servings)

You can improve your eating habits by planning ahead. List your favorite foods from each group.

- ◆ **Bread, Rice, Cereal, and Pasta** ____________
- ◆ **Vegetables** ____________
- ◆ **Fruit** ____________
- ◆ **Milk, Yogurt, and Cheese** ____________
- ◆ **Meat, Poultry, Fish, Beans, Eggs, and Nuts** ____________
- ◆ **Fats, Oils, and Sweets** ____________

Unit 2 • Managing Yourself 17

Pages 18–19

- **You Can Make Healthy Choices**
  Ask a volunteer to read each tip aloud. Then invite students to share ideas for adding exercise to their daily routines, as well as ideas for healthy snacks. Demonstrate how the healthy habits students begin now will last throughout their lives by sharing some ways you incorporate healthy activities into your own life (see *Teacher Modeling*).
- **Eat Like an Athlete**
  You Are *When* You Eat
  Encourage students to try eating a diet rich in foods from the bottom of the food pyramid. Suggest that students keep a food/mood log for several weeks. Since the results won't be apparent right away, periodically ask students how the experiment is working.
- **Where Are You Going?**
  Ask students to write a goal that will help them lead a healthier life in the future.

Teacher Modeling

You may wish to use or adapt these examples of teacher modeling.

To stay healthy:

- I take time to eat a good breakfast before work—usually cereal, a banana, and orange juice.
- I ride my bike or walk to do errands whenever I can.
- I keep a container of water on my desk to drink when I'm thirsty.
- I eat three well-balanced meals a day.
- I eat fruit for a snack instead of candy or chips.
- I wash my hands before meals, especially during cold and flu season.
- I try to get eight hours of sleep every night.
- I don't smoke or use drugs that aren't prescribed by my doctor.

You Can Make Healthy Choices

Exercise, Exercise, Exercise!

Work exercise into your daily routine whenever you can. Regular physical exercise keeps your muscles and heart in good shape. It can also reduce stress, tension, and anxiety. It may not be as hard as you think to find ways to exercise. You can do stretches even while you're sitting down. And sometimes you can walk or ride your bike instead of asking for a ride in the car. Even cleaning up your room is good exercise!

The Eyes Have It

Eyestrain can give you a headache. It also makes it hard for you to concentrate. Always read and work under a good light. Natural light and incandescent lighting are better for your eyes than fluorescent lighting. If you get headaches or have trouble concentrating when you read, ask for an eye test.

Healthy Snacks

Remember the food guide pyramid? It can help you plan healthy snacks. We should all eat three to five servings of vegetables a day and two to four servings of fruit. Remember that it's just as easy to snack on a carrot or some fruit as it is to grab a candy bar. It's better for you, too!

Take Care of Those Teeth

Brush your teeth at least twice a day. If possible, carry a toothbrush so you can brush after every meal. Healthy teeth and gums are important for many reasons. Did you know that infected teeth and gums can cause serious health problems? An infection that starts in your mouth can travel to other parts of your body.

Turn a Frown Upside Down

Keep smiling! Smiling is much easier than frowning. Did you know that it takes only about seventeen muscles to smile? When you frown, you use forty-three muscles.

A positive attitude is very healthy.

Water, Water Everywhere

Drink eight glasses of water a day to keep your body working at its best. Soft drinks and fruit juices don't count. You really need to drink plain old water!

18 **Level C** • Achieve Mastery

Eat Like an Athlete

Research shows that athletes who eat starchy, carbohydrate-rich diets have better endurance than athletes on high protein diets.

The ideal diet for an athlete includes potatoes, whole grain noodles, rice, bread, beans, peas, raw or steamed vegetables, and small amounts of meat, eggs, and milk. This diet is low in butter, sugar, and other fattening foods.

If you get lots of exercise, an athlete's diet might give you more energy. Try adding more carbohydrates to your diet for a short period of time. See if you have extra energy.

Carbohydrates are a main source of fuel for the muscles and the brain.

You Are *When* You Eat

Even if you eat a healthy diet, you may find yourself feeling tired, grouchy, or unable to concentrate at certain times of the day. Your diet can cause these feelings. Too much sugar at one time may cause you to feel very energetic for a while. But when the sugar wears off, you may feel extremely tired, or even sad and depressed. A big meal may taste good, but you may feel sleepy afterward. Sometimes you may not even realize that you're hungry. If you find you can't concentrate, a healthy snack may help.

To see how eating affects your moods, try keeping a food/mood log. Write down everything you eat and the time you eat it. Whenever your mood changes, write it in the log. See if you can find a pattern or a connection between your food intake and your moods. Even if you can't control the times when you eat, you'll often be able to control what you eat and how much you eat.

Where Are You Going?

Summarize what you learned in this lesson. ______________________

____

____

Now use your summary to write a ***Take Charge!*** goal that will help you become a better student.

____

____

Unit 2 • Managing Yourself 19

Managing Distractions

About Distractions

It's natural for students to get distracted while studying. Even the quietest study areas have distractions like people talking, telephones ringing, or music playing. One key to academic success is understanding how to work through distractions. This lesson will show students how to improve their concentration and use their time more efficiently by controlling the distractions in their study environment.

Pages 20–21

◆ **Distractions Are Everywhere! Where Do You Stand?/Rate Yourself**
After students read the lesson introduction, invite them to discuss similar experiences they've had. Ask how they dealt with the distractions. Then give students an opportunity to assess their ability to manage distractions by completing the quiz.

◆ **Distractions, Distractions**
Most students will think of distractions they hear, such as people talking, a barking dog, or loud music. Encourage them to add distractions they can see, touch, taste, or smell. As students work together, they may be surprised to find that things that distract some of them don't bother others at all. Encourage less distractible students to share their strategies for maintaining concentration. Discuss some of your own strategies for managing distractions (see *Teacher Modeling*).

◆ **Take Control**
Ask students to list steps for controlling distractions. Encourage students to implement the changes over the next week. Make one student responsible for initiating a follow-up discussion after students have had a chance to put their ideas into practice. During the discussion, ask students to tell whether their school performance improved and what techniques worked best.

5 LESSON

Managing Distractions

STAY TUNED FOR . . .

R-r-ring! R-r-ring! Leesa, telephone!

Arf! Arf! Arf!

Distractions Are Everywhere!

You're all set to study. You've got your books and materials together. You've enjoyed a snack. You've changed into comfortable clothes. You've planned your whole evening, and you're even looking forward to getting your math homework out of the way and completing a long social studies project.

But things don't go quite the way you planned. The doorbell rings, and then your cousin who lives out of town calls. The cat sits on your papers, and the dog won't stop barking until you play fetch. When you finally get to work, you can't keep yourself from listening to the TV show that's on in the next room.

Does this sound familiar? Everyone's life is full of distractions. You just need to learn how to deal with them.

Where Do You Stand?

What would you do in these situations? Circle the approach you think would work best for you.

Situation 1:
It's late afternoon. You're doing your homework. A friend calls and wants to get together. What do you do?

a. Finish your homework quickly so you can meet your friend later.
b. Meet your friend and do your homework later.
c. Tell your friend that you need to study, but you'd like to get together another day.
d. Tell your friend you can't get together, then chat on the phone for an hour.

Situation 2:
You have a big test tomorrow, and there's a great movie on television. What do you do?

a. Review your notes during commercials.
b. Watch the movie and then stay up as late as you can to study for your test.
c. Rent the movie from the video store and watch it another night.
d. Do your studying quickly so you have time to watch the second half of the movie.

20 Level C • Achieve Mastery

Rate Yourself

If you chose answer *c* for both questions, you know how to stick to a task. If you chose any other answers, you sometimes let distractions get in the way of doing your best work. Read on to learn how to get control of the distractions in your life.

Distractions, Distractions

What is distracting for one person may be soothing background noise for another person. For most people, though, the fewer distractions you have, the better you concentrate and the more efficiently you work.

In a small group, brainstorm a list of things that can be distracting when you're trying to study. Consider physical distractions in your environment that you can see, hear, touch, taste, or smell, and mental distractions inside your own head. Write your ideas below. Then reread your list and star the distractions that are most annoying to you.

Take Control

Make a list of at least five specific steps you could take to reduce distractions in your study environment. For example, your list might include making a rule for yourself, such as *No TV while studying!* or hanging a *Do Not Disturb* sign on the bedroom door.

Do Not Disturb

Put the ideas on your list into practice for the next two weeks. Keep track of your school performance during this time. If your schoolwork improves, you'll know that your study environment has been affecting your school performance. It would be smart to incorporate these distraction reducers into your regular study routine.

Unit 2 • Managing Yourself 21

Pages 22–23

◆ **Quiet, Please!**
Make Use of "White" Noise
Music Can Make You Smarter
Ask volunteers to read the tips. Allow time for students to try the memorization experiment. Explain that researchers are studying "The Mozart Effect"—the idea that listening to Mozart's compositions can boost brain power.

◆ **Get Rid of Inner Distractions**
Find the Best Place to Study
Talk Over the Problem
Read the tips with students. Emphasize that, while students can control many distractions on their own, there may be times when they need help from others. If time allows, students can role-play situations in which they ask for help from friends and family members.

◆ **Where Are You Going?**
Ask students to write a goal to help them control distractions as they study.

Teacher Modeling

You may wish to use or adapt these examples of teacher modeling.

To avoid distractions while reading:

- I keep a sheet of paper handy to write down distracting thoughts. I can deal with these ideas after I finish reading.
- I set reading goals, such as reading five pages in five minutes.
- After reading for half an hour, I take a short break and stretch or walk around.
- If noise distracts me, I move to a quieter place or turn on a fan to cover the sounds.

To avoid distractions while working with others:

- I look directly at the person speaking and focus on his or her facial expressions and gestures.
- I make a group to-do list and check off tasks as they are completed.

Tips for Dealing With Distractions

Quiet, Please!

Studying in a quiet place might improve your grades. Comprehension rates usually decrease in direct proportion to the amount of sound in your environment. Try this experiment to find out how noise affects you.

Find a short poem. Memorize the first half of the poem with loud music or noise in the background. Spend as much time as you need to be able to write the lines perfectly from memory. Make a note of how much time you spent. Then turn off the music and find a quiet place to memorize the other half of the poem. Again, time yourself. Compare the amounts of time you spent memorizing each half of the poem. Did distracting noises affect your concentration?

Make Use of "White" Noise

If you find that noise affects you, you can sometimes turn off the sound and work in a quiet place. But some noises, like street or family sounds, cannot be turned off. In that case, you might be able to cover the sounds with "white" noise. White noise is bland, repetitive noise like the hum of a fan or rain falling on the roof. Your mind soon gets used to the sound of white noise and tunes it out. Since you're close to the source of the noise, it can hide louder sounds that are farther away.

Get Rid of Inner Distractions

In addition to physical distractions in your environment, "inner noise" can also interrupt your concentration. Inner noise is made up of thoughts, worries, and daydreams that keep running through your mind. It can be every bit as disturbing as noise from outside sources. It's hard to turn off your inner noise, but you need to do it if you're going to be able to concentrate. Tell yourself to focus on one thing at a time. Promise yourself that you'll think, worry, and daydream later.

Try this technique for clearing your mind. When you sit down to study, take a moment to calm yourself. Keep a blank sheet of paper handy. Write down thoughts that are taking up your attention. Get them out of your head and onto the paper. Whenever new distracting thoughts intrude, add them to your list. You can deal with them when you've finished your studying.

Music Can Make You Smarter

Some kinds of music have the same effect as white noise. Try tuning your radio to an "easy listening" station that plays soft music without sudden loud tones or distracting lyrics. Or listen to classical music. Studies have shown that certain pieces of classical music help your mind focus. Classical music can even make you work "smarter."

Try listening to classical music when you study. You might find it helps you concentrate.

22 Level C • Achieve Mastery

Find the Best Place to Study

Some places have built-in distractions. You can't always expect everything to stop just because you want to study. Your family may not be willing to turn off the television just because you plan to study for a test in the living room. And if you have brothers or sisters, they probably won't be quiet on command! You may need to change your own study schedule to cut out distractions.

If your usual study space has too many distractions, be creative. Can you study in the library after school or at an after-school homework center? Is there a corner of a bedroom you could turn into your own special study spot at certain times? Some people even use a closet for their own private "office."

QUIET!
KATE'S SECRET STUDY ZONE
KEEP OUT!
SSHH!!

Talk Over the Problem

Don't be afraid to discuss the problem of distractions with friends, family members, or your school counselor. Let your friends know when your scheduled study times are. Ask them to call at a different time or to be understanding when you say you will call them back later. Your family members may be able to come up with ideas you haven't even thought of for providing a quiet time or a new place for you to study. And a counselor or teacher may be willing to let you study in an empty classroom or may know of an after-school program you weren't aware of. Once you make up your mind to be more focused on your studies, you may be surprised how much others are willing to help.

Where Are You Going?

Summarize what you learned in this lesson. ______________________

____

____

Now use your summary to write a ***Take Charge!*** goal that will help you become a better student.

____

____

Unit 2 • Managing Yourself 23

Identifying Strengths and Weaknesses

About Strengths and Weaknesses

A key factor in success is knowing yourself well. And a big part of knowing yourself is understanding your strengths and weaknesses. Since adolescence is itself a period of change and self-discovery, this lesson comes at an appropriate time in students' lives. Students will evaluate their assets. Then they'll learn ways to build on their strengths and compensate for weaknesses.

Pages 24–25

◆ **Meet These Best Friends**
Students can read the introduction to find out about the strengths of the girls in the picture. In a follow-up discussion, help students categorize the girls' strengths as academic, organizational, and people skills, or teamwork. Suggest that students write their name and the names of two friends and write one strength beside each name.

◆ **Where Do You Stand?/Rate Yourself**
Imagining their reactions to different situations will help students assess their strengths. After students complete the quiz, encourage them to rate themselves to see whether their quiz results match their own ideas about their areas of strength.

◆ **Role Models**
Take Inventory
To help students clarify the concept of different kinds of strengths, invite them to work in groups to name people who have demonstrated special skill in each area. Ask groups to share the names of their role models with the class and explain why they chose each person. Once they understand each area of strength, they will be ready to take inventory of their own strengths. Demonstrate how students can put their self-knowledge to work by sharing some ways you capitalize on your strengths and work around your weaknesses (see *Teacher Modeling*).

6
LESSON

Identifying Strengths and Weaknesses

Tina likes to peer tutor younger students. Rachel is head of the school's can food drive. Jackie is captain of the field hockey team.

Meet These Best Friends

Tina, Rachel, and Jackie are best friends, yet they are involved in very different activities. Tina has strong academic skills. She has an ability to learn new things quickly. That's why she volunteers to help other students. Rachel is an organizer. She can manage multiple tasks and coordinate large projects. Jackie is good at motivating people. She has the ability to work well with her teammates.

All three girls are capitalizing on their strengths. Everyone has different strengths and weaknesses. What are yours?

Where Do You Stand?

Just like Tina, Rachel, and Jackie, all people are stronger in some situations and weaker in others. Read the situations below. Circle *Strong* or *Weak* to show how you'd feel about handling each situation.

1. It's time to take a big test in your favorite subject.
   Strong Weak
2. Your best friend's dog died, and he feels very sad.
   Strong Weak
3. Your little sister got into your room and pulled everything off the shelves. What a mess! How will you ever get everything back together?
   Strong Weak
4. Your teacher has asked you to tutor a new student.
   Strong Weak
5. Your two best friends are having an argument. They say they'll never speak again.
   Strong Weak
6. Your club is organizing a charity food drive and you've been asked to lead the project.
   Strong Weak

24 Level C • Achieve Mastery

Rate Yourself

There are many different kinds of skills and talents. You may be strong in academics, music, art, organizational skills, or in working with people. The quiz assesses your skills in three areas: academics, people skills, and organization. If you circled *Strong* for questions 1 and 4, you feel that academics is a strength. If you circled *Strong* for questions 2 and 5, people skills may be your strength. If you circled *Strong* for 3 and 6, your organizational skills are probably strong.

Role Models

Everyone has strengths and weaknesses. That doesn't mean that one person is better than another. It simply means that people learn and perform activities in a variety of ways based on their strengths.

In a small group, brainstorm a list of people that you know who are particularly strong in the areas listed below. These people can be classmates, family members, or famous people. After you have listed several people in each category, discuss what skills they possess that make them good at what they do.

People with strong organizational skills

____

____

People with strong academic skills

____

____

People with strong skills in working with other people

____

____

Take Inventory

Take inventory of your own strengths and weaknesses. For each category below, list activities that you feel you have accomplished successfully. Don't worry if you don't have a long list in every category.

Organizational tasks

Academic tasks

Tasks working with other people

Are you better at some types of tasks than others? Once you understand what comes naturally to you, you can develop strategies to help you capitalize on your strengths and minimize your weaknesses.

Unit 2 • Managing Yourself 25

Pages 26–27

◆ **Capitalize on Your Strengths**
Ask a volunteer to read each section aloud. Since the emphasis during students' lives has mostly been on academics, those who don't excel in this area may feel they don't have strengths. Many students will be reassured to know that organizational skills and people skills are highly valued in the workplace and in life. Ask students to brainstorm other skills that are valued outside of school.

◆ **Learning Strengths**
Ask students to give examples of ways to use each mode in different learning situations.

◆ **Assess Yourself**
As students respond to the questions, remind them that it's important to work to improve those areas that are not currently strengths.

◆ **Where Are You Going?**
Ask students to write a goal that will help them make better use of their strengths.

Teacher Modeling

You may wish to use or adapt these examples of teacher modeling.

At work:

- I use my academic strengths to decide what students need to know and the best ways to help them learn.
- I use my organizational strengths to make sure I accomplish my goals.
- I use teamwork, or people skills, to work with both my colleagues and my students.

When I volunteer for a project:

- I choose roles that will let me use my strengths.
- I keep lists of resources that can help me with more challenging parts of the job.

When a task I need to do doesn't fit my strengths:

- I look for a way to use my strengths.
- I work extra hard on the parts that I know are my weaknesses.

Capitalize on Your Strengths

Different Kinds of Strengths

People have many different kinds of strengths. They may have special talents in music and art, academics, athletics, working with people, or organizing. You may have strengths in more than one area and weaknesses in more than one area.

Since you've been a student most of your life, the emphasis has probably been on your academic strengths. Your ability to learn is an important skill you will use all your life. But as you leave school to go to work, you'll find that employers also value teamwork, or people skills. Teamwork skills include being a leader, doing your part to carry out your group's goals, and getting along with others.

Employers also value personal management and organizational skills. These skills range from the ability to get to work on time to a talent for setting up a plan for accomplishing goals within a time frame.

Learning Strengths

Your strengths are reflected in the ways you learn. Some people learn best by listening. Some learn best by seeing. And some learn best by touching or moving things around. How do you learn best?

Auditory Mode: People who learn best by listening are *auditory learners*. You may be an auditory learner if you remember the tunes and lyrics of songs easily. Auditory learners generally find it easy to remember what their teachers say in class.

Visual Mode: People who learn best by seeing are *visual learners*. If you easily remember what you read, you may be a visual learner. Can you close your eyes and picture the details of something you've only seen a few times? Then you may be a visual learner, too. Most painters and photographers are visual learners.

Tactile or Kinesthetic Mode: People who learn best by touching or doing are *tactile* or *kinesthetic learners*. Do you have to write down a telephone number before you can remember it? Then your learning strength may be tactile. If you like to work on crafts or perform science experiments, you're probably a kinesthetic learner. Dancers who remember complicated sequences of steps are often kinesthetic learners.

Make it your goal to develop strengths in these three areas: ability to learn, teamwork, and personal management and organization.

Compensating for Weaknesses

There are two ways to approach weaknesses. One is to work hard to turn your weakness into a strength. If you have trouble organizing, improve this skill by making lists and schedules.

The other is to try to compensate for a weakness by using a strength. If you're a tactile learner in a lecture class, turn what you hear into good written notes. The act of writing will burn the ideas into your brain. If you are a visual learner, take notes in the form of webs or pictures whenever possible.

Working to Your Strengths

Once you become aware of your strengths, find ways to use them whenever you can. If people skills are your strength, organize a study group before the next test. If you're an auditory learner, make an audiotape of your social studies notes to learn them.

The most important thing is to learn to like the person you are and the strengths you have. The next time you face a challenge, like a big test or a major project, you'll feel ready to use your strengths to tackle it head on!

Assess Yourself

Think about what you've learned about strengths. Then write a brief answer for each of the following questions.

1. Is your ability to learn one of your strengths? How could you improve your learning skills?
____
2. Do you like to work on teams? How could you improve your teamwork skills?
____
3. Are you well organized? Do you manage time well? How could you improve your personal management and organizational skills?
____
4. What is your strongest learning mode: auditory, visual, or tactile/kinesthetic? Why do you think you learn best in this mode?
____

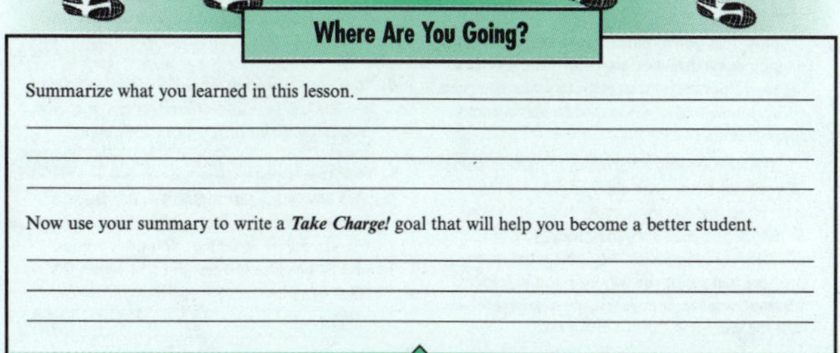

Where Are You Going?

Summarize what you learned in this lesson. ______________________

Now use your summary to write a ***Take Charge!*** goal that will help you become a better student.

____

Resisting Negative Influences

About Negative Influences

Most middle school students feel a strong need to belong to a peer group. They also have a well-developed sense of right and wrong. But when their sense of right and wrong conflicts with the actions of their peer group, good judgment may be pushed into the background. In this lesson, students will learn strategies for resisting negative influences that might distract them from their academic and life goals.

Pages 28–29

- **Who Are Your Friends?**
  Ask a volunteer to read the lesson introduction. Then initiate a discussion about setting goals and making decisions. Invite volunteers to describe people they trust to help them make different kinds of decisions.
- **Where Do You Stand?/Rate Yourself**
  After students take the quiz, reread the questions together, pointing out that they all involve school-related activities. Guide students to think about the motives of peers who try to convince them that doing well in school isn't "cool." Reinforce the idea that school success leads to lifelong success and that sticking to personal goals is the "coolest" thing they can do.
- **Stand Up for Yourself**
  Saying *No*
  Ask students to work on their own to list their favorite strategies for saying *no* to peers who are pressuring them. Then organize students into groups to share strategies and describe situations in which they might need to use them. If time allows, ask each group to develop a role-play for one of their situations and perfom it for the class. During a follow-up discussion, tell students that negative influences won't go away as they grow older. Share some techniques you use to resist negative peer pressure (see *Teacher Modeling*).

7 LESSON

Resisting Negative Influences

Who Are Your Friends?

Now that you're older, you're responsible for making some decisions on your own. But it's a big world out there! It's tough to make decisions all by yourself. You need good friends around to support you.

You've probably noticed, though, that some of your old friends are changing. Some may even be trying out things you think are wrong or dangerous. And they may want you to try those things along with them. Negative peer pressure can get in the way of good judgment. It's important to choose friends who want the best for you.

Where Do You Stand?

How good are you at resisting negative peer pressure? Take the quiz below to find out. Read each statement and mark the scale to show how often you respond this way.

1. You have a Spanish test last period. At lunch, you take a copy of the test offered from a friend who took the test in the first period.
   Hardly Ever ① ② ③ ④ ⑤ Almost Always
2. You know you have to practice for your recital. A friend asks you to go to the movies so you do that instead.
   Hardly Ever ① ② ③ ④ ⑤ Almost Always
3. You don't raise your hand to answer questions in class anymore because your friends laughed at your answer the last time.
   Hardly Ever ① ② ③ ④ ⑤ Almost Always
4. You have a brother who did the same science project last year and offered to give it to you. You copy it and turn it in as your own.
   Hardly Ever ① ② ③ ④ ⑤ Almost Always
5. You have a big test tomorrow. But there is a television show on late tonight that all your friends will be watching. You need a good night's sleep for the test but you watch the show anyway.
   Hardly Ever ① ② ③ ④ ⑤ Almost Always

28 **Level C** • Achieve Mastery

Rate Yourself

To rate your resistance to negative peer pressure, add up the numbers in the circles you filled in. Write your total in the box.

- If you scored under 8, congratulations! You are taking control of your own actions. Read on for more helpful tips.
- If you scored between 8 and 16, you might be letting your friends influence you a little too much. You can improve your decisions by trying some of the strategies in this lesson.
- If you scored over 16, you may need to rethink how you choose and interact with your friends.

Stand Up for Yourself

It's natural to be curious about new activities, but most people understand that some things are just plain wrong. What things are wrong? Well, things that are unhealthy or illegal are wrong. And sometimes the things that get in the way of reaching your goals are wrong.

Often it's enough just to avoid people who have different values. But once in a while you're likely to find yourself alone in a group of people who think differently than you. When that happens, saying *no* can be hard. The key to saying *no* is planning ahead.

On the lines below, write your best strategies for avoiding going along with the crowd.

Saying *No*

Saying *no* is a skill. Like most skills, it takes practice. Form a small group with two other classmates. Make up three situations in which someone your age might need to say *no*. Describe the situations on the lines below.

Situation 1:

Situation 2:

Situation 3:

Now role-play the situations and demonstrate ways to say *no*. Take turns being the people who are pressuring and the person who is saying *no*. Use techniques you wrote about earlier or make up new ones as you go along. Choose your best skit and act it out for the class.

Unit 3 • Working With Others 29

Pages 30–31

- **Tips for Managing Peer Pressure**
  Invite volunteers to read the tips aloud. Pause after each tip to ask for student comments and examples. After reading *Can We Talk?*, ask students to brainstorm a list of resources available in your school or community.
- **Ways to Say *No***
  After reading the different ways to say *no,* ask students to compare them to the strategies they listed on page 29. You may wish to compile a class list of ways to resist peer pressure. If time allows, provide sample situations, such as those given in the *Where Do You Stand?* quiz on page 28, and ask students to suggest or act out appropriate ways to say *no*.
- **Where Are You Going?**
  Ask students to use what they've learned to write a goal to help them resist negative influences in the future.

Teacher Modeling

You may wish to use or adapt these examples of teacher modeling.

When friends pressure me to do something I don't want to do:

- I tell them I'm not interested.
- I suggest an alternative activity.
- I try to change their minds if I'm afraid the activity will get my friends in trouble.

When I'm in a situation that doesn't feel quite right:

- I trust my instincts.
- I leave.

To plan ahead:

- I ask lots of questions before I commit to a situation.
- I rehearse in my mind ways to say *no* if a friend suggests an activity that doesn't match my values.

Tips for Managing Peer Pressure

Choose Your Friends Wisely

There's an old saying you've probably heard from your parents: *You are judged by the company you keep.* This means that if you hang around with people who act in a certain way, other people will think you believe the actions are okay. You need to choose your friends wisely. As you grow up, you'll keep some of your old friends, and you'll also make new ones. Remember that a friend is not just someone who lives nearby or someone you've always known. A friend is a person who cares about you. It's a person who doesn't always have to be the boss, a person who listens to what you say and accepts your feelings. If your friends won't take no for an answer, you probably have the wrong friends.

You are judged by the company you keep.

Can We Talk?

When you're having problems with peer pressure, don't be afraid to ask for advice. You can talk to friends your own age. You can also talk to family members, teachers, counselors, or people you know from community activities. Choose a person you trust, and choose your words carefully. Speak in general terms if you want to. That means you don't need to name names—you can say "a classmate" or "someone I know."

Choose Your Battles

Sometimes you can solve a problem just by avoiding the person who is pressuring you or by walking away. Sometimes you may want to take the time and trouble to explain your feelings or to try to talk your friend out of whatever he or she is planning.

What you decide to do may depend on the seriousness of the situation. If you think your friend is getting into real trouble, you may decide to try to convince your friend that the action is wrong. If you're not sure, you can ask a trusted adult to help you decide.

Keep Your Goals in Mind

There are different kinds of peer pressure. A friend may try to pressure you into doing something like going to a movie instead of doing your homework. Or, a friend may try to pressure you into doing something more serious like skipping school, smoking, or using alcohol and other drugs. Just keep your personal goals in mind and consider the consequences of your decisions. Make the decisions that lead you toward a healthy, happy, and productive future.

When choosing your friends, be sure to keep your personal goals in mind.

30 **Level C** • Achieve Mastery

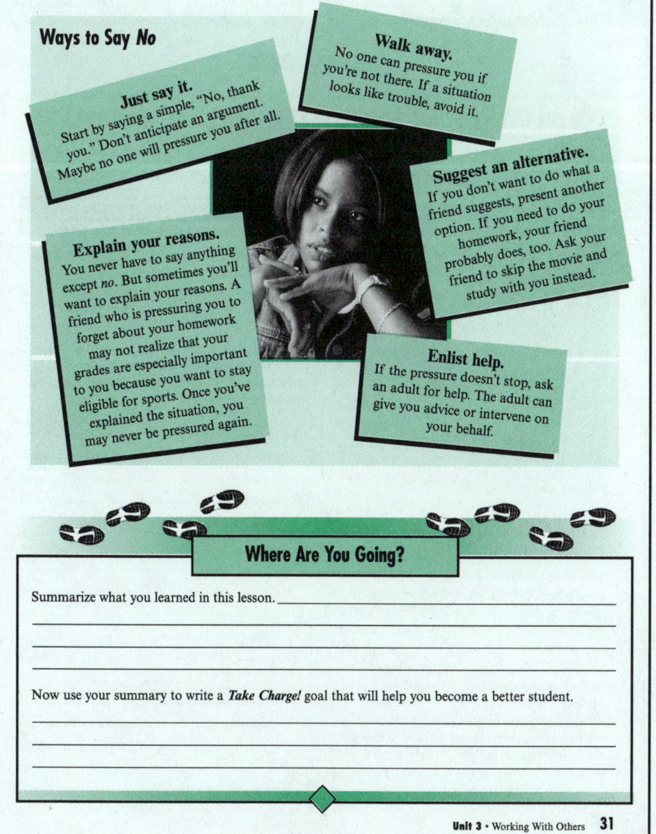

Ways to Say *No*

Just say it.
Start by saying a simple, "No, thank you." Don't anticipate an argument. Maybe no one will pressure you after all.

Walk away.
No one can pressure you if you're not there. If a situation looks like trouble, avoid it.

Explain your reasons.
You never have to say anything except *no*. But sometimes you'll want to explain your reasons. A friend who is pressuring you to forget about your homework may not realize that your grades are especially important to you because you want to stay eligible for sports. Once you've explained the situation, you may never be pressured again.

Suggest an alternative.
If you don't want to do what a friend suggests, present another option. If you need to do your homework, your friend probably does, too. Ask your friend to skip the movie and study with you instead.

Enlist help.
If the pressure doesn't stop, ask an adult for help. The adult can give you advice or intervene on your behalf.

Where Are You Going?

Summarize what you learned in this lesson. ______________________

Now use your summary to write a ***Take Charge!*** goal that will help you become a better student.

____

Unit 3 • Working With Others 31

Solving Problems in a Group

About Group Problem Solving

Many students enjoy working as part of a group. Besides being a social experience, working with others to solve a problem can stimulate a wealth of ideas and make a long, difficult job easier by splitting the responsibilities among several people. But group members sometimes have difficulty working together, and then problems and conflicts often occur. In this lesson, students will learn strategies for keeping a group running smoothly, both in school and out.

Pages 32–33

- **Join the Team**
  After students read the introduction, ask them to point out problems the group in the picture seems to be having. Students may say that one girl is dominating the group, and another is asleep. One boy looks angry, while another looks puzzled. Another girl is crossing her arms and leaning back in an attempt to withdraw from the group.

- **Where Do You Stand?/Rate Yourself**
  After completing the quiz, students will see that group problem solving is part of their everyday lives, not just a school exercise. Invite them to give examples from previous group experiences to explain their responses to the poll in *Rate Yourself*.

- **Work on Your Own**
  Work With a Group
  Compare the Processes
  These activities serve two purposes. First, students are asked to give advice to address real problems they might encounter during group work. Second, solving similar problems in different ways gives students a basis for comparing individual work with teamwork. As students work together to write advice, circulate and observe the interaction of each group. Afterward, share your observations, along with some of your own tips for working in groups (see *Teacher Modeling*).

---

8 LESSON

Solving Problems in a Group

Teamwork is fun when it works. But sometimes a team needs a little coaching.

Join the Team

Solving problems can be tricky. And working with a group to solve a problem or complete a project can be even trickier. Differences of opinion and uncooperative behavior can make the time some groups spend together frustrating and unproductive.

You probably already recognize the symptoms of "sick group syndrome." It happens when some group members dominate the conversation, some joke around or disrupt the group, and others just tune out. The good news is that there are strategies you can learn to help make group work more productive and a lot more fun.

Where Do You Stand?

You probably make more group decisions than you realize. A group can be anything from yourself and one other person to a whole classroom. In both cases, you need to work together.

Below is a list of places in which you spend part of your school day. For every location, describe a situation in which you need to solve a problem in a group.

1. Gym ______
2. Lunchroom ______
3. Classroom ______
4. School bus ______
5. Hallway ______

32 **Level C** • Achieve Mastery

Rate Yourself

Think about the group problem-solving situations you described. Do you enjoy making decisions in a group or would you rather decide on your own? Take a poll to see how many students in your class enjoy group work and how many have had negative experiences with group work.

Work on Your Own

Whether or not you like group work, you will face many situations that require you to work with others. Everyone can learn and practice strategies to make group work go more smoothly. Use your own experiences with group work to give advice to the student below. Work by yourself to write your advice.

Four of us are in the middle of an important social studies project. We have to be ready to present it to the class next week. The project—and the grade—are really important to me. Unfortunately, there's this one guy in our group who keeps clowning around. I'd like to just tell him off—but when other members of the group do that, he actually seems to enjoy it. What do I do?

Work With a Group

Now form a group with three or four classmates. Read the problem below and write some advice. This time, work together to find a solution everyone in the group agrees on.

A group of us are planning a dance. When we got together last week, I had as many ideas as anyone, but no one seemed willing to listen. If these weren't my friends, I'd probably just quit.

Compare the Processes

Which advice was easier to write—the advice you wrote alone or the advice you wrote in a group? Why?

Unit 3 • Working With Others 33

Pages 34–35

- **Six Basic Steps**
  Students can follow this plan for tackling most problems. You may want to post the steps in the room so students can refer to them whenever they work in groups.
- **Set Standards**
  Groups can head off potential problems by establishing standards of behavior at the first meeting. Emphasize that when groups work together to set standards, all members are likely to follow them.
- **Assign Jobs**
  Another way to ensure the participation of every group member is to assign each one a specific responsibility. Students can adapt the jobs list to fit their group's particular purpose.
- **Where Are You Going?**
  Ask students to write a goal including group problem-solving techniques they plan to try.

Teacher Modeling

You may wish to use or adapt these examples of teacher modeling.

When I work with a group to solve a problem:

- I keep in mind that all group members are important because we all bring special skills to the team.
- I help establish standards and then make sure to follow them.
- I say what I think, but I think before I speak.
- I make sure my comments are helpful and to the point.
- I listen respectfully when another group member is speaking.
- I am polite to other group members, even when we disagree.
- I perform the jobs the group assigns me to the best of my ability.

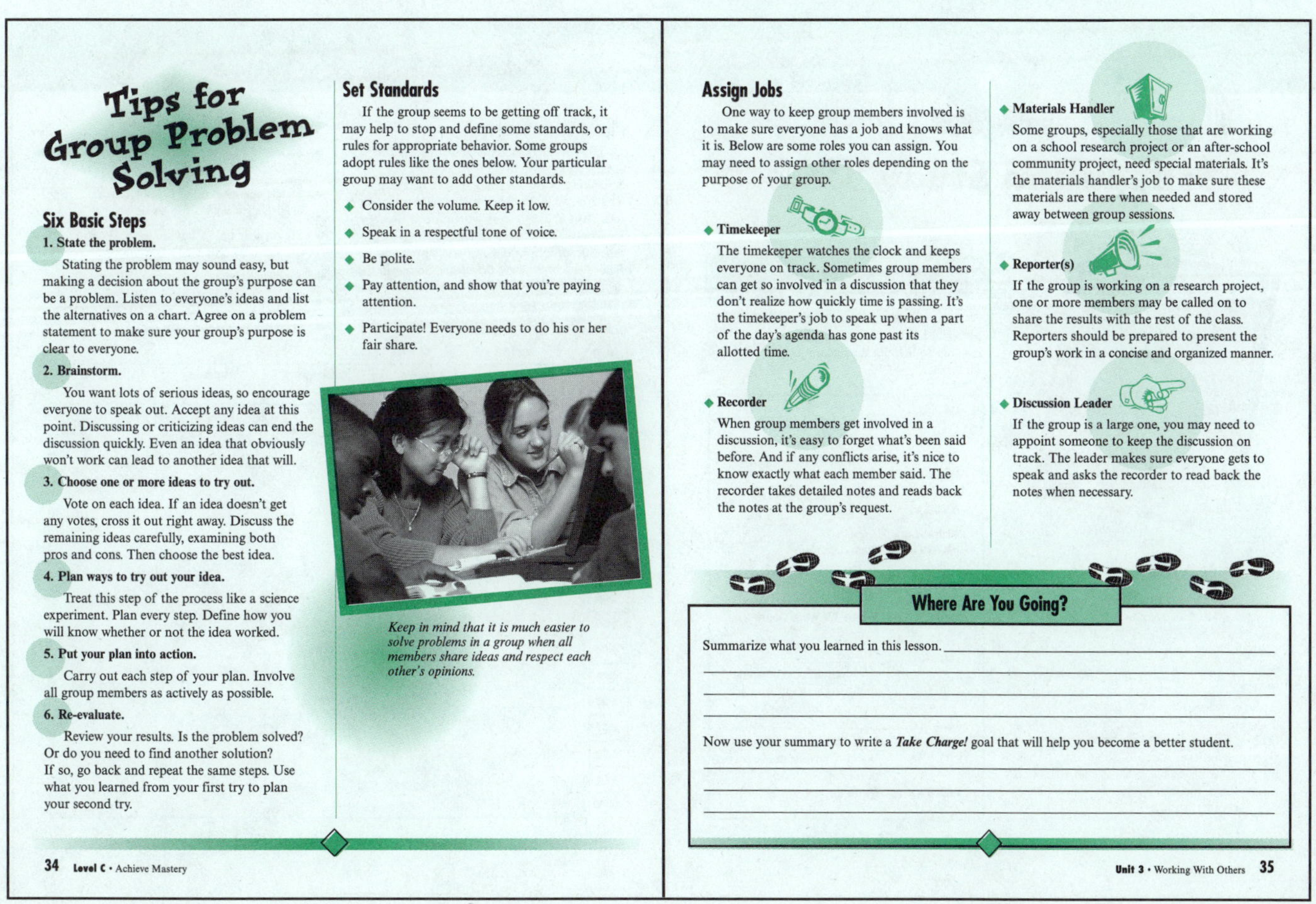

Tips for Group Problem Solving

Six Basic Steps

1. State the problem.

Stating the problem may sound easy, but making a decision about the group's purpose can be a problem. Listen to everyone's ideas and list the alternatives on a chart. Agree on a problem statement to make sure your group's purpose is clear to everyone.

2. Brainstorm.

You want lots of serious ideas, so encourage everyone to speak out. Accept any idea at this point. Discussing or criticizing ideas can end the discussion quickly. Even an idea that obviously won't work can lead to another idea that will.

3. Choose one or more ideas to try out.

Vote on each idea. If an idea doesn't get any votes, cross it out right away. Discuss the remaining ideas carefully, examining both pros and cons. Then choose the best idea.

4. Plan ways to try out your idea.

Treat this step of the process like a science experiment. Plan every step. Define how you will know whether or not the idea worked.

5. Put your plan into action.

Carry out each step of your plan. Involve all group members as actively as possible.

6. Re-evaluate.

Review your results. Is the problem solved? Or do you need to find another solution? If so, go back and repeat the same steps. Use what you learned from your first try to plan your second try.

Set Standards

If the group seems to be getting off track, it may help to stop and define some standards, or rules for appropriate behavior. Some groups adopt rules like the ones below. Your particular group may want to add other standards.

- Consider the volume. Keep it low.
- Speak in a respectful tone of voice.
- Be polite.
- Pay attention, and show that you're paying attention.
- Participate! Everyone needs to do his or her fair share.

Keep in mind that it is much easier to solve problems in a group when all members share ideas and respect each other's opinions.

34 **Level C** • Achieve Mastery

Assign Jobs

One way to keep group members involved is to make sure everyone has a job and knows what it is. Below are some roles you can assign. You may need to assign other roles depending on the purpose of your group.

- **Timekeeper**
  The timekeeper watches the clock and keeps everyone on track. Sometimes group members can get so involved in a discussion that they don't realize how quickly time is passing. It's the timekeeper's job to speak up when a part of the day's agenda has gone past its allotted time.
- **Recorder**
  When group members get involved in a discussion, it's easy to forget what's been said before. And if any conflicts arise, it's nice to know exactly what each member said. The recorder takes detailed notes and reads back the notes at the group's request.
- **Materials Handler**
  Some groups, especially those that are working on a school research project or an after-school community project, need special materials. It's the materials handler's job to make sure these materials are there when needed and stored away between group sessions.
- **Reporter(s)**
  If the group is working on a research project, one or more members may be called on to share the results with the rest of the class. Reporters should be prepared to present the group's work in a concise and organized manner.
- **Discussion Leader**
  If the group is a large one, you may need to appoint someone to keep the discussion on track. The leader makes sure everyone gets to speak and asks the recorder to read back the notes when necessary.

Where Are You Going?

Summarize what you learned in this lesson. ______________________

Now use your summary to write a ***Take Charge!*** goal that will help you become a better student.

____

Unit 3 • Working With Others 35

Scheduling Study Time

About Scheduling

Even the most disciplined students often have difficulty making the best use of their time. Given the choice between having fun with their friends and studying for a test that is a whole week away, it's natural for students to choose fun and friends. In this lesson, students will learn the benefits of using time-management skills to schedule the time they need to prepare for tests. By consulting their schedules, they'll be able to see at a glance what activities they can do without jeopardizing their chances for a good test grade.

Pages 36–37

◆ Meet Joe
Where Do You Stand?

As students read the lesson introduction, they may realize that they know someone like Joe. They may even be able to recall times when they have been guilty of taking a "laid-back" approach to studying for a test, and suffered the consequences of a poor grade. Suggest that students use what they've learned from their experience to help Joe revise his schedule in *Where Do You Stand?* Ask volunteers to share their revisions of Joe's schedule. The new schedules should include a block of test-study time each evening. Share your own strategies for scheduling time to prepare for a big event (see *Teacher Modeling*).

◆ Plan a Study Strategy
Scheduling Secrets

Remind students to use the points in *Scheduling Secrets* as guidelines for filling in the test-study schedule. If possible, have students plan for an upcoming test. Or, if necessary, invent a hypothetical test students should plan for. Suggest that students critique their completed schedules in small groups. During a follow-up discussion, invite students to share what they learned about short- and long-term planning.

Meet Joe

Believe it or not, Joe is usually happy and easygoing. His friends know him as the guy who likes to make plans at the last minute and somehow finds a way to "get by" in his schoolwork. Joe doesn't seem to take anything very seriously.

So why does Joe look so unhappy? He just discovered that a laid-back approach isn't always the best strategy, especially when it comes to preparing for tests. Joe spent some time studying the night before the big social studies test, but it was too little, too late. No wonder he isn't happy with his grade!

Where Do You Stand?

Read how Joe spent the three nights before his test. Cross out and rewrite parts of the schedule to help Joe do a better job of studying for his test.

Tuesday
- 3:30–5:00 Play ball with friends
- 5:00–6:00 Listen to new disc while doing homework
- 6:00–6:30 Eat dinner
- 6:30–7:30 Talk on the phone
- 7:30–9:45 Watch a movie

Wednesday
- 3:30–4:00 Piano lesson
- 4:00–6:00 Watch soccer game at school
- 6:00–6:30 Eat dinner
- 6:30–8:00 Play video game at friend's
- 8:00–9:45 Watch TV while doing homework

Thursday
- 3:30–4:30 After-school club meeting
- 4:30–6:00 Call friends to talk and ask what's on tomorrow's test
- 6:00–7:00 Eat dinner; clean up kitchen
- 7:00–8:00 Help Mom with groceries
- 8:00–9:00 Watch TV while doing homework
- 9:00–9:45 Cram for test

36 **Level C** • Achieve Mastery

Plan a Study Strategy

Use the calendar below to plan a week of special study sessions for an upcoming test. Schedule at least one study session each day. Think about all the ways you know to study for a test. Do you like to work with a friend? Recopy your notes? Make flash cards? Allow time in your schedule for all your favorite study methods. Before you begin, read *Scheduling Secrets* in the next column. They'll help you make a test-prep plan that really works!

Scheduling Secrets
- ◆ Schedule fixed time blocks first, such as your class schedule.
- ◆ Determine what other time blocks are available for possible study time.
- ◆ Set realistic time estimates for study time during these time blocks.
- ◆ Set clear starting and stopping times.
- ◆ Schedule time for short breaks.
- ◆ Be sure to schedule some time for fun each day.

	Monday _/_/_	Tuesday _/_/_	Wednesday _/_/_	Thursday _/_/_	Friday _/_/_
7:00					
8:00					
9:00					
10:00					
11:00					
12:00					
1:00					
2:00					
3:00					
4:00					
5:00					
6:00					
7:00					
8:00					
9:00					
10:00					

Unit 4 • Studying for Tests 37

Pages 38–39

- **Tips for Scheduling Study Time**
  Ask students to read the tips on their own. The four-day plan is just an example. Students planning for their own tests may have more or fewer days to study. The suggestions in *Three, Two, One, Test Time!* are common-sense strategies for feeling relaxed and prepared on test day. Ask volunteers to summarize long-term and short-term steps they can take to prepare for tests.
- **The Pros and Cons of Cramming**
  It may be difficult to convince students that cramming is not the best way to study. Use the list of pros and cons to discuss why waiting until the last minute is not the best way to prepare for a test.
- **Where Are You Going?**
  Ask students to write a goal that will help them schedule study time for future tests.

Teacher Modeling

You may wish to use or adapt these examples of teacher modeling.

When I have an important event to plan for:

- I begin my planning early.
- I list the things I need to accomplish and the amount of time I think each will take.
- I review my schedule every day to make sure I'm following it as closely as I can.

On the day before the big event:

- I make sure I've completed everything on my schedule.
- I go to bed early so I'll be sure to get plenty of sleep.

On the day of the big event:

- I wake up in time to eat a healthy breakfast.
- I make sure I have all the materials I'll need.
- I give myself time to get where I need to go.

Tips for Scheduling Study Time

Plan Ahead

Postponing your studying until the day before the test is like preparing for an athletic competition by exercising for one day. If you haven't been working out all along, you're not in shape, and one day's exercise won't help. The way to make sure you're in tip-top test-taking shape is to manage your time to allow for daily study and review.

Review your notes every day, whether there's a test coming up or not. Make sure your daily schedule allows at least fifteen minutes to review each of your subjects. Divide your daily reviews into two parts. Use half of your review time to reread information you've learned in the last day or week. Use the rest of your time to memorize facts like names, dates, definitions, and equations.

You can't push back the hands of time. Make sure you are ready for tests by scheduling daily study and review. Begin your serious studying four or five days before a test.

Ready, Set, Study!

DAY 1

On the first day, just skim your notes, homework assignments, and quizzes. Look for gaps in the information. If you find any, fill them in by reading your textbook or asking your teacher or a classmate for help.

DAY 2

On the second day, skim all the test material. Recite important ideas out loud to yourself and make sure you can explain each idea clearly.

DAY 3

On the third day, read over your notes. Write key words and ideas in the margins. Make flash cards. Then, without looking at the rest of your notes, say aloud to yourself the details that go with each key word or main idea.

DAY 4

On the fourth day, use your notes to make up a sample test and test yourself, or have someone quiz you on your notes. If you're doing well at this point, give yourself a short break. If you don't do so well on your practice test, repeat the quizzing process until you're sure you understand all the important ideas and have memorized the facts you need to know to explain the ideas. Practice tests will make the real thing feel like no big deal.

38 Level C • Achieve Mastery

The Pros and Cons of Cramming

You may hear some people say that they never study until the night before a test. Trying to get all your studying done in one marathon study session is called "cramming." If you think cramming is a good idea, read the Pros and Cons below. Then decide for yourself.

PROS:

- You stuff a lot of studying into a little bit of time.
- You might pass the test.

CONS:

- You'll probably forget what you studied as soon as the test is over.
- You won't have the knowledge base you'll need to learn new things in the future.
- You're likely to feel stressed and nervous on the day of the test.
- All the time you spent in class was wasted.
- You might not pass the test.

Three, Two, One, Test Time!

Start getting psyched up for a big test on the night before. Review the material you've been studying for the past several days and then relax and get a good night's sleep. In the morning, eat a good breakfast, do a little exercise to get your blood flowing, and take a shower to get your brain in gear. If you have time, go over the material briefly once again. Put on some comfortable clothes, gather everything you'll need for the test, and say to yourself, "I'm a winner!"

Get to class early. On your way to the classroom, go to the restroom and get a drink of water. Get comfortable in your seat and settle in. Clear your desk of unnecessary items, sit straight up in your chair, and take a few deep breaths. Then relax until the test begins—you're ready for success!

Assess Yourself

Look back at the schedule you planned on page 37. Now that you've studied these tips, are there any changes you'd like to make? If so, make the adjustments now.

Where Are You Going?

Summarize what you learned in this lesson. ________________

Now use your summary to write a ***Take Charge!*** goal that will help you become a better student.

____

Unit 4 • Studying for Tests 39

Monitoring Your Test Readiness

About Self-Monitoring

Most students agree that good study habits are linked with successful school performance. But without some way of monitoring their progress, students often think they are meeting requirements when, in fact, they are falling short. In this lesson, students will learn strategies for getting the most from their study time. When they put these self-monitoring strategies into effect, they'll find that they perform better on tests and other assignments. The result will not only be better grades, but also increased levels of confidence and decreased levels of stress.

Pages 40–41

- **Do You Know What You Know?**
  Discuss the definition of *self-monitoring* and the importance of keeping track of one's own progress instead of relying on someone else to do it. After students read the introduction, continue the discussion by sharing your own strategies for self-monitoring (see *Teacher Modeling*).
- **Where Do You Stand?/Rate Yourself**
  Students can begin evaluating their self-monitoring skills by taking the quiz.
- **Are You Ready?**
  Let small groups list facts they might find on a review test for one of their classes, or brainstorm a class list of facts students must know for an upcoming test. Guide students as they sort the facts into the two categories on the chart. Remind students to refer to the *Study Strategies* listed and to add their own favorite strategies. Ask volunteers to tell how they used self-monitoring to complete the chart.

Pages 42–43

- **Review, Review, Review**
  Test Yourself
  Point out that when good students have a few extra minutes, they review in their heads. This gives them an idea of what they need to learn.

10 LESSON

Monitoring Your Test Readiness

I thought I knew this.

Do You Know What You Know?

As you study for tests, do you feel that you have a pretty good idea of what you understand and what you need to spend more time on? Knowing how well you're doing is called *self-monitoring*. It means keeping track of your own progress.

Successful students monitor their progress while they study. This helps them decide what steps to take next—whether to go over difficult material again, try a different study strategy, or ask for help. Some students monitor themselves automatically, but those who don't can learn how.

Where Do You Stand?

How good are you at self-monitoring your test readiness? Complete the questionnaire below to find out. Read the statements and think about what you do when you have a test. Fill in the circle that shows how often you do each thing.

1. I feel confident while I'm taking a test.
   Hardly Ever ① ② ③ ④ ⑤ Almost Always
2. During class and when I'm studying, I ask myself questions to make sure I understand the material.
   Hardly Ever ① ② ③ ④ ⑤ Almost Always
3. As I study, I stop periodically to test myself.
   Hardly Ever ① ② ③ ④ ⑤ Almost Always
4. I make checklists to make sure I haven't forgotten anything.
   Hardly Ever ① ② ③ ④ ⑤ Almost Always
5. I use different methods—such as flash cards or revising my notes—to study different kinds of information.
   Hardly Ever ① ② ③ ④ ⑤ Almost Always
6. I review tests I've taken to find ways I could have improved my scores.
   Hardly Ever ① ② ③ ④ ⑤ Almost Always

40 Level C • Achieve Mastery

Rate Yourself

To rate your skills, add up the numbers in the circles you filled in. Write your total in the box.

- If you scored over 24, congratulations! You already use some self-monitoring as you study.
- If you scored between 15 and 23, you sometimes monitor your own test readiness, but you can become more aware of what you do and don't know.
- If you scored below 15, you may have trouble knowing when you're ready for a test. By learning to monitor your test readiness, you'll be a more successful and confident test-taker.

Are You Ready?

Aggh! One of your teachers just announced that in two weeks there will be a review test over everything you have studied in class so far this year. How will you prepare?

Get together with two or three others who have the same class as you. Look through your textbook and notes and brainstorm some facts you might find on a review test for that class. Then fill in the chart below. In the top, write sample facts you might find on the test—some facts you think you already know and some you need to learn. In the lower part, write some ways you might review or learn those facts for the test. Use the study strategies at right for some ideas.

Facts I Think I Know	Facts I Don't Know
Study Strategies	Study Strategies

Study Strategies
- flash cards
- revise/recopy notes
- study group
- outlines, webs, and graphic organizers
- mnemonic devices
- practice tests
- recite out loud
- checklists

Unit 4 • Studying for Tests 41

Until this process becomes automatic, students can make paper-and-pencil tests to help them know what they know and what they need to learn.

- **Join Study Groups**
  Check It Off
  These tips help students gain a realistic perspective. In study groups, students see how their progress measures up to that of others. They also have a chance to exchange study strategies and use successful students as role models. Students who prefer to study alone can measure their progress against a checklist.
- **Live and Learn**
  Many students forget all about a test once they've taken it, especially if the grade was lower than they had hoped. If possible, ask students to answer the questions as they review a test they've taken recently.
- **Where Are You Going?**
  Ask students to write a goal that will help them monitor their own study progress.

Teacher Modeling

You may wish to use or adapt these examples of teacher modeling.

When I am faced with a complicated task:

- I make a checklist of things to do and learn.
- I include everything I can think of on my checklist and I add to it whenever new things come up.
- I check things off the list as I do them.

To monitor my progress:

- I test myself from time to time or review my checklist.
- I talk about my progress with others so I can compare my progress with theirs.

To improve my performance:

- I assess the work I've already done.
- I think about what I have learned from my previous mistakes.

Tips for Monitoring Yourself

Review, Review, Review

You'll always be ready for a quiz or a test if you constantly review. Don't just read over your notes and stop. Analyze what you know and don't know. Ask yourself whether you could explain the main ideas to someone who has never heard them before. See which facts and details you can rattle off without taking time to think about them. Make a list of things you still don't understand. Then reread your notes and textbook or ask questions. When you feel confident about your knowledge, cross the item off your list.

Test Yourself

Every once in a while, stop to make up a sample test for yourself. Try to make it as much like the tests your teacher gives as possible. Create questions that test your knowledge of main ideas and details and questions that force you to make connections and apply what you've learned. Then take your self-made test to see how you're doing.

Join Study Groups

If you're the kind of person who likes to study with friends, you already know how useful the give-and-take between members of a study group can be. But even if you usually prefer studying alone, studying occasionally with a group can give you some useful guidelines for monitoring your test readiness. You can measure your progress against that of other group members on a regular basis. And you and the other members of the group can help each other out—after all, everyone has different weaknesses and strengths.

Try having each group member write some questions about different sections of the material, or have everyone in the group write a sample test for the whole group to take. Work together to decide what the group members need to learn at the next study session.

When forming a study group, remember that it is important to keep all members involved. Be respectful of everyone in the group and you will benefit from each other's ideas.

Check It Off

Make a checklist for each subject. Then, as you prepare to take a test, use your checklist the way astronauts use preflight checklists before blasting off. After all, as every astronaut knows, once you're in space it's too late to correct something you forgot to check. Your pretest checklist can help you monitor yourself. You can see whether you've prepared for every kind of question that might appear on the test.

Begin your checklists on the very first day of class and add to them as the year goes on. Include page numbers of reading assignments, dates of class notes, problems you'll need to solve, and skills you'll have to master. Include major ideas, definitions, theories, formulas, and equations as separate items on your checklists. When it comes time to prepare for a big test, check each item off the list as you master it.

Live and Learn

When your teacher returns your corrected test, don't just take a quick peek at the grade, groan, and hide the test away somewhere. Take a close look at it with these questions in mind:

- What kinds of questions did my teacher ask? Which kind gave me the most trouble?
- What material did the test focus on—class notes, textbooks, or homework exercises? Was it the material I concentrated on as I studied?
- What did I do best on the test?
- What study strategies helped me the most?
- What changes do I need to make to do better the next time?

Where Are You Going?

Summarize what you learned in this lesson. ____________________

Now use your summary to write a ***Take Charge!*** goal that will help you become a better student.

____

Techniques for Memorizing

About Memorizing

To succeed in school, students need to be able to memorize facts, formulas, rules, dates, and other information. This lesson will teach students some mnemonic devices, memory aids named after Mnemosyne, the Greek goddess of memory. These memory aids will help make the information students learn in school unforgettable. Mnemonic devices in this lesson include visual links, acronyms, sayings, and rhymes.

Pages 44–45

◆ **Memory Matters**
Where Do You Stand?/Rate Yourself
After students read the lesson introduction, suggest that they move right on to the quiz. As students rate their answers, discuss how they memorize historical events, scientific facts, and other information. Share some of your own strategies for memorizing important information (see *Teacher Modeling*).

◆ **Think Like Cicero**
Encourage students to close their eyes and take an imaginary walk through the school, picturing items from the list in different rooms. The giraffe might be greeting visitors in the office, and the lake might be in the cafeteria. Then students can cover the list with a blank sheet of paper and test their memory. If they forget some of the objects, suggest that they repeat the process.

◆ **How Do You Spell It?**
Let small groups work together to make memory aids for words they choose from the box. Explain that the tricky parts of these words are underlined and that their mnemonics should focus on these parts. If you prefer, have students create memory aids for content-area words or for words they personally find troublesome. Create a class list of spelling memory tricks. Then hold an old-fashioned spelling bee so students can show what they've learned.

11
LESSON

Techniques for Memorizing

One of the most famous speakers in ancient Rome was Cicero. Cicero used a special trick to remember his speeches.

Memory Matters

How did the famous Roman orator Cicero remember his speeches? He didn't use index cards or TelePrompTers. Cicero associated parts of his speeches with parts of his home. The opening of the speech might have been linked with his bed chamber, the next part with his yard. As he progressed through the speech, Cicero mentally took a walk through the rooms in his house.

Succeeding in school depends on remembering things like dates, math and science formulas, historical events, characters, and plots. There are two basic ways to memorize. One is by repetition—reading or saying something over and over until you know it "by heart." The other is what Cicero did—linking new ideas to something familiar. You can link what you're trying to remember with images and words that are so silly you just can't forget them or with images and words that are already familiar. Learning new strategies for making memory links will save you time when you memorize. It can even be fun!

Where Do You Stand?

You probably already use memory links, or *mnemonic* (ni MON ik) *devices.* Do the words and phrases below look familiar? Each one is a mnemonic device. Write an explanation for each one that you know.

1. HOMES
2. When two vowels go walking, the first vowel does the talking.
3. My Uncle Steve can lift elephants.
4. My very excellent mother just served us nine pizzas.

Rate Yourself

Read the answers to see how you did. If some of the memory links were unfamiliar, use them now to remember the facts.

1. HOMES is an acronym that helps us remember that the five Great Lakes are Huron, Ontario, Michigan, Erie, and Superior.
2. When you were just beginning to read, you may have learned this rhyme to remember that the first vowel in a pair is usually the one you pronounce. Can you think of an example?
3. This sentence helps you remember how to spell the word *muscle*.
4. This sentence helps you list the planets in our solar system in order of distance from the sun: Mercury, Venus, Earth, Mars, Jupiter, Saturn, Uranus, Neptune, Pluto.

Think Like Cicero

Remember Cicero's memory trick? He pictured a familiar place and put one thing he wanted to remember in each room. Try the same idea to remember a nonsense list. Picture the items on the list below in different places in your school. Then cover the list, take an imaginary walk, and write what you remember on the lines below.

giraffe, lake, pencil, daisy, automobile, mountain, football, book, tree, fence

How Do You Spell It?

Some words are just plain confusing. You could practice spelling them over and over and still make a mistake. Mnemonic devices, or memory links, can help you. Here are a few examples of memory tricks for spelling.

principal (of your school)—The principal is my pal.
principle—The principle is the rule.
acquaint—I will seek you (CQ) out to get acquainted.
bargain—You gain from a bargain.

There are many other troublesome words. Here are some examples:

separate	comfortable	occur
address	bureau	foreign
potatoes	commitment	environment

Work with a small group of classmates to create memory links for three of the troublesome words above. Write your ideas below.

Pages 46–47

- **Add Memory Power**
  Remind students that their mnemonic devices don't need to be works of art. Anything that works for them is "correct." This is one time it's okay to be silly. Silly images and sayings are often more memorable. Let students share their creations. If necessary, give some sample answers. To make a link, they might draw an image of President George Washington carving statues of sweet potatoes and peanuts. One example of a silly sentence that will help them remember Presidents Ford, Carter, Reagan, Bush, and Clinton is *Four cats ran beside Charlie*.
- **Memorizing Tips**
  Conclude by inviting volunteers to read aloud the general tips for memorizing.
- **Where Are You Going?**
  Ask students to write a goal for using mnemonic devices to improve their memory.

Teacher Modeling

You may wish to use or adapt these examples of teacher modeling.

To help me remember:

- I link facts with silly images I just can't forget.
- I make my mind a camera and take a "snapshot" of a formula or diagram, so I can picture it later.
- I make up sentences whose words begin with the same letters as the things I'm memorizing. To remember the first five presidents, I use the sentence *Who angered Jeff's mad monster?* (Washington, Adams, Jefferson, Madison, Monroe)
- To memorize information about a historical event, I imagine myself in that time and place.
- To memorize people's names, I link a physical characteristic with a name. For example, Nancy (Nan-SEE) wears glasses to help her see.

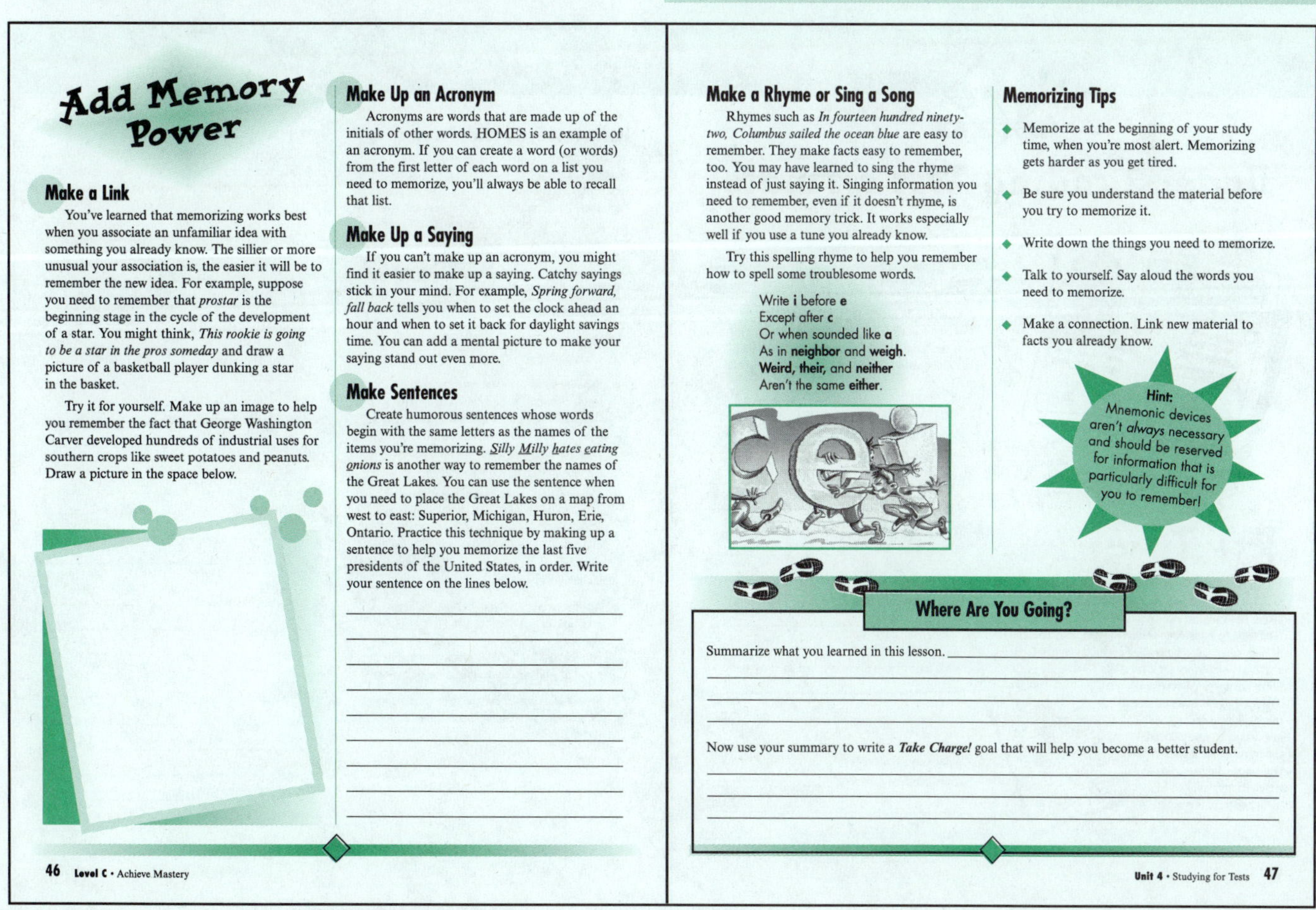

Add Memory Power

Make a Link

You've learned that memorizing works best when you associate an unfamiliar idea with something you already know. The sillier or more unusual your association is, the easier it will be to remember the new idea. For example, suppose you need to remember that *prostar* is the beginning stage in the cycle of the development of a star. You might think, *This rookie is going to be a star in the pros someday* and draw a picture of a basketball player dunking a star in the basket.

Try it for yourself. Make up an image to help you remember the fact that George Washington Carver developed hundreds of industrial uses for southern crops like sweet potatoes and peanuts. Draw a picture in the space below.

Make Up an Acronym

Acronyms are words that are made up of the initials of other words. HOMES is an example of an acronym. If you can create a word (or words) from the first letter of each word on a list you need to memorize, you'll always be able to recall that list.

Make Up a Saying

If you can't make up an acronym, you might find it easier to make up a saying. Catchy sayings stick in your mind. For example, *Spring forward, fall back* tells you when to set the clock ahead an hour and when to set it back for daylight savings time. You can add a mental picture to make your saying stand out even more.

Make Sentences

Create humorous sentences whose words begin with the same letters as the names of the items you're memorizing. *Silly Milly hates eating onions* is another way to remember the names of the Great Lakes. You can use the sentence when you need to place the Great Lakes on a map from west to east: Superior, Michigan, Huron, Erie, Ontario. Practice this technique by making up a sentence to help you memorize the last five presidents of the United States, in order. Write your sentence on the lines below.

46 Level C • Achieve Mastery

Make a Rhyme or Sing a Song

Rhymes such as *In fourteen hundred ninety-two, Columbus sailed the ocean blue* are easy to remember. They make facts easy to remember, too. You may have learned to sing the rhyme instead of just saying it. Singing information you need to remember, even if it doesn't rhyme, is another good memory trick. It works especially well if you use a tune you already know.

Try this spelling rhyme to help you remember how to spell some troublesome words.

Write **i** before **e**
Except after **c**
Or when sounded like **a**
As in **neighbor** and **weigh**.
Weird, their, and **neither**
Aren't the same **either**.

Memorizing Tips

- Memorize at the beginning of your study time, when you're most alert. Memorizing gets harder as you get tired.
- Be sure you understand the material before you try to memorize it.
- Write down the things you need to memorize.
- Talk to yourself. Say aloud the words you need to memorize.
- Make a connection. Link new material to facts you already know.

Hint: Mnemonic devices aren't *always* necessary and should be reserved for information that is particularly difficult for you to remember!

Where Are You Going?

Summarize what you learned in this lesson. ______

Now use your summary to write a *Take Charge!* goal that will help you become a better student.

Unit 4 • Studying for Tests 47

Understanding Test Formats

About Test Formats

Most students know it's important to study material they expect to find on a test. But they may not realize the importance of understanding different test formats and purposes. Students who fail to use the best strategies for answering different kinds of questions may not test well, even when they know the material well. In this lesson, students will learn to recognize different test formats and purposes. They will also learn test-taking strategies that will help them succeed under all kinds of testing conditions.

Pages 48–49

- **Test Time**
  Read the introduction with your students. Then discuss different kinds of tests students are likely to encounter in their lives and what their purposes are. Model the importance of understanding test formats by sharing strategies you have used to pass different kinds of tests (see *Teacher Modeling*).
- **Where Do You Stand?**
  After students complete the quiz, take a survey to compare students' feelings about different kinds of test questions. Encourage students to give reasons for their feelings and to suggest answers for questions 4 and 5.
- **Understand Every Test's Purpose**
  Test Talk
  Suggest that students work in small groups to read and discuss the definitions of different kinds of tests and to think of examples from their own experience. In a follow-up discussion, invite volunteers to tell what they have learned from taking different tests and how they have used the results.

Pages 50–51

- **Know Your Test Strategies**
  Invite volunteers to read the tips aloud.

---

12 LESSON

Understanding Test Formats

You've passed lots of tests in your life, and you'll need to pass even more.

Test Time

You've already taken lots of tests in your life as a student, and you're sure to be taking many more, both in and out of school. You need to take tests to pass your classes, to get your driver's license, to get into college or technical school, and maybe even to get a job. Different types of tests are designed to find out different things. Therefore, it's very important to understand the purpose of a test. When you know the purpose, you have a better chance of giving correct answers.

Where Do You Stand?

An attitude inventory is designed to help you understand your feelings and preferences. Think about the kinds of questions on the tests you take. Then answer the questions in this attitude inventory.

1. What kind of question—true-false, multiple-choice, matching, short-answer, or essay—do you think is the easiest? Why? ______
2. What kind of test question do you think is the hardest? Why? ______
3. Which kind of test question do you usually do well on? Why? ______
4. What would you do to change the way tests are given? ______
5. What ways besides tests can you think of to assess student progress? ______

Understand Every Test's Purpose

Different kinds of tests have different purposes. Listed below are five types of tests you will probably encounter. Read the descriptions of each test. Understanding what a test can mean to you gives you an incentive to study and perform your best.

- **Classroom tests** measure how much you've learned in a few days or weeks, a school term, or an entire school year. Because classroom tests occur so often, they help you know where you stand in your classes and what you need to study.
- **Standardized tests, or norm-referenced tests,** compare achievement level with a statistical sample of other students. These tests let you know where you rank in a group of students your age from all over the United States who have taken the same test.
- **Criterion-referenced tests** measure what you know without comparing you with other students. They tell you which skills you've mastered and which ones you still need to work on. If you take a state proficiency test, it's probably a criterion-referenced test.
- **Aptitude tests** analyze your skills, abilities, and interests. When it's time for you to choose a career, an aptitude test can help you learn what type of work you might be good at and what you might enjoy.
- **Entrance exams** measure your qualification for admission to special programs or schools.

Test Talk

In a small group, review the five types of tests and their purposes. Then work together to think of examples of each kind of test you've taken. Describe them on the lines below.

1. Classroom test ______
2. Standardized test ______
3. Criterion-referenced test ______
4. Aptitude test ______
5. Entrance exam ______
6. Other tests ______

Pause after each one so students can add tips of their own. You may want to spend extra time on analogies, which often appear on standardized tests. Ask students to write a few analogies with a partner, using vocabulary words or material from a content-area text. Let the class practice completing the analogies.

- **Ready, Set, Go!**
  Remind students that knowing about different test formats does not make up for a lack of studying. No matter what kinds of questions are on a test, students can prepare ahead of time by organizing materials as they receive them. Encourage students to begin to organize now so they'll be ready to use their new test-taking strategies when their next major test comes around.
- **Where Are You Going?**
  Ask students to write a goal that includes using knowledge about different kinds of tests to improve their test scores.

Teacher Modeling

You may wish to use or adapt these examples of teacher modeling.

When I need to prepare for a test:

- I motivate myself by thinking about the purpose of the test.
- I study the material the test will cover.
- I ask what kinds of questions will be included on the test.

To answer short-answer questions:

- I answer all the questions I'm sure about first.
- I answer with specific facts and details.

To answer essay questions:

- I read the question carefully to make sure I understand it.
- I make an outline and write my answer just as if I were writing a longer essay or report.
- I include plenty of details and examples.

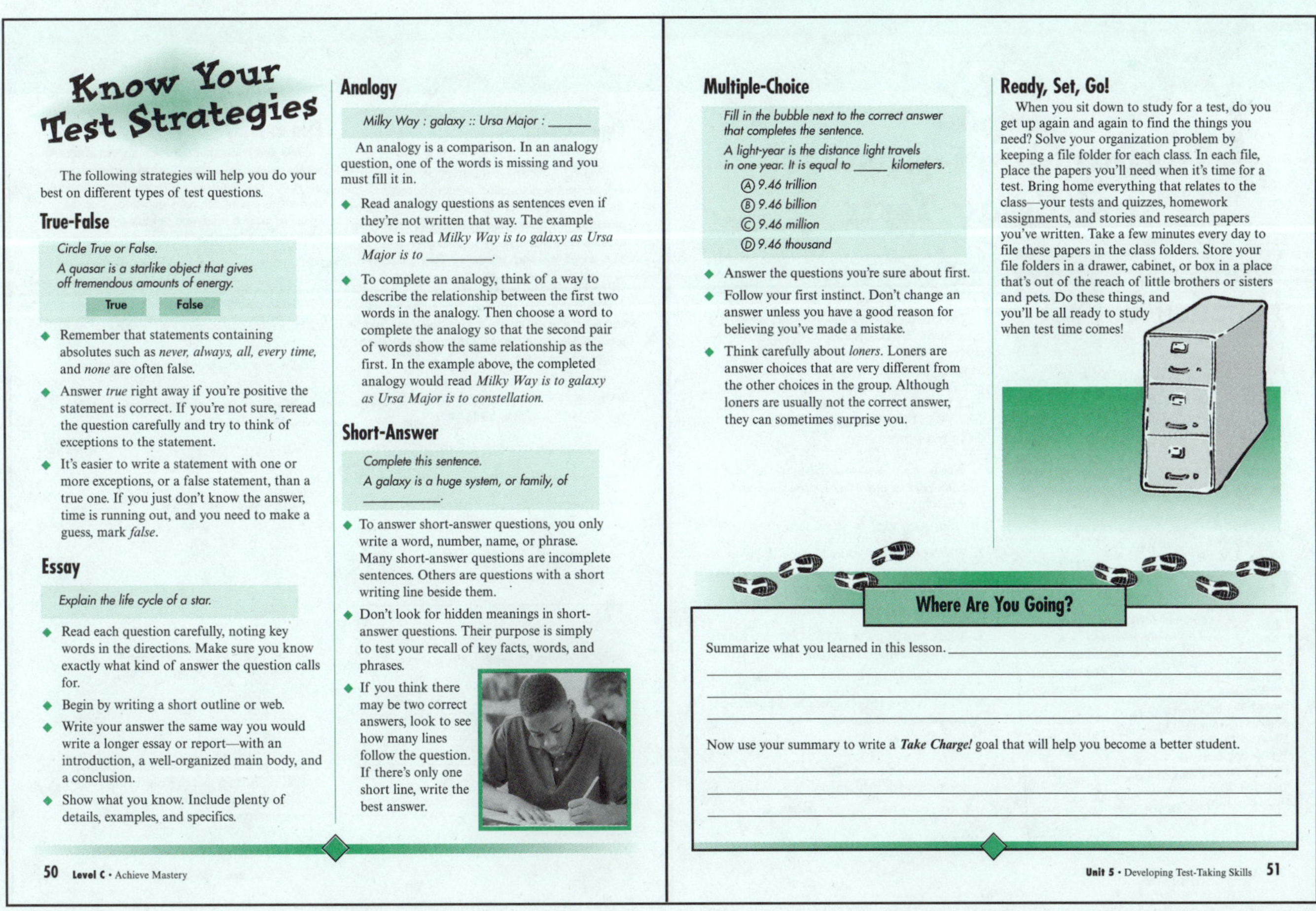

Know Your Test Strategies

The following strategies will help you do your best on different types of test questions.

True-False

Circle True or False.
A quasar is a starlike object that gives off tremendous amounts of energy.
True False

- Remember that statements containing absolutes such as *never, always, all, every time,* and *none* are often false.
- Answer *true* right away if you're positive the statement is correct. If you're not sure, reread the question carefully and try to think of exceptions to the statement.
- It's easier to write a statement with one or more exceptions, or a false statement, than a true one. If you just don't know the answer, time is running out, and you need to make a guess, mark *false*.

Essay

Explain the life cycle of a star.

- Read each question carefully, noting key words in the directions. Make sure you know exactly what kind of answer the question calls for.
- Begin by writing a short outline or web.
- Write your answer the same way you would write a longer essay or report—with an introduction, a well-organized main body, and a conclusion.
- Show what you know. Include plenty of details, examples, and specifics.

Analogy

Milky Way : galaxy :: Ursa Major : ______

An analogy is a comparison. In an analogy question, one of the words is missing and you must fill it in.

- Read analogy questions as sentences even if they're not written that way. The example above is read *Milky Way is to galaxy as Ursa Major is to* ________.
- To complete an analogy, think of a way to describe the relationship between the first two words in the analogy. Then choose a word to complete the analogy so that the second pair of words show the same relationship as the first. In the example above, the completed analogy would read *Milky Way is to galaxy as Ursa Major is to constellation.*

Short-Answer

Complete this sentence.
A galaxy is a huge system, or family, of __________.

- To answer short-answer questions, you only write a word, number, name, or phrase. Many short-answer questions are incomplete sentences. Others are questions with a short writing line beside them.
- Don't look for hidden meanings in short-answer questions. Their purpose is simply to test your recall of key facts, words, and phrases.
- If you think there may be two correct answers, look to see how many lines follow the question. If there's only one short line, write the best answer.

50 Level C • Achieve Mastery

Multiple-Choice

Fill in the bubble next to the correct answer that completes the sentence.
A light-year is the distance light travels in one year. It is equal to _____ kilometers.
Ⓐ 9.46 trillion
Ⓑ 9.46 billion
Ⓒ 9.46 million
Ⓓ 9.46 thousand

- Answer the questions you're sure about first.
- Follow your first instinct. Don't change an answer unless you have a good reason for believing you've made a mistake.
- Think carefully about *loners.* Loners are answer choices that are very different from the other choices in the group. Although loners are usually not the correct answer, they can sometimes surprise you.

Ready, Set, Go!

When you sit down to study for a test, do you get up again and again to find the things you need? Solve your organization problem by keeping a file folder for each class. In each file, place the papers you'll need when it's time for a test. Bring home everything that relates to the class—your tests and quizzes, homework assignments, and stories and research papers you've written. Take a few minutes every day to file these papers in the class folders. Store your file folders in a drawer, cabinet, or box in a place that's out of the reach of little brothers or sisters and pets. Do these things, and you'll be all ready to study when test time comes!

Where Are You Going?

Summarize what you learned in this lesson. ______________________________

Now use your summary to write a ***Take Charge!*** goal that will help you become a better student.

Unit 5 • Developing Test-Taking Skills 51

Taking Short-Answer and Essay Tests

About Short-Answer and Essay Tests

Many students who breeze through multiple-choice tests freeze when asked to generate answers on their own. They dread short-answer questions, which require quick recall of facts. And they often don't know where to begin with essay questions, which require them not only to remember details and main ideas but also to organize information and write an answer in a short time. In this lesson, students will learn strategies for generating responses to short-answer and essay questions. This knowledge will help students perform better on tests and make tests less intimidating.

Pages 52–53

- **Words of Experience**
  Choose volunteers to read the letters aloud. Explain that even though essay tests and short-answer tests seem different, they are related because both require students to think of the answers on their own. Share strategies you've used while taking short-answer and essay tests (see *Teacher Modeling*).
- **Where Do You Stand?/Rate Yourself**
  Students can take the quiz to see how well they already understand short-answer and essay tests.
- **How to Tackle Tests**
  Allow time for students to brainstorm study methods for different kinds of tests and write their group's best ideas. Groups may wish to share their strategies with the whole class.
- **Plan an Essay**
  Before students begin, explain that students are not being asked to actually write an essay, and don't need to research any facts. Suggest that they choose the topic they know the most about and write main ideas they would include or questions they would need to answer if they were really writing the essay.

13 LESSON

Taking Short-Answer and Essay Tests

Words of Experience

Dear Testmaster,

Essay tests terrify me! True-false, multiple-choice, analogies, and even short-answer or fill-in-the-blank tests are a breeze. There are usually enough clues in the questions to help me remember the answers. But an essay test is too much like a blank sheet of paper. Not only do I have to know what I'm writing about, I also have to think of a way to write what I know in a clear and organized way. And all that in one class period! Is that fair?

Terrified in Toledo

Dear Terrified in Toledo,

Yes, it's fair. In fact, essay tests are the best way for you to show what you know. When you've studied hard, learned the information you need to know, and mastered the basic writing skills that you use for any writing assignment, you can relax. Essay tests won't be a problem. Don't be afraid of expressing your own ideas and opinions. Just remember to back up your thoughts with supporting facts and details that prove your point. Your teacher will know that you've mastered the information—and that you know how to think for yourself!

The Testmaster

Where Do You Stand?

Do you feel like Terrified in Toledo when your teacher announces a test with short-answer or essay questions on it? Relax! If you understand the purpose of these tests, it will help ease your fears about taking them. See how much you already know about essay and short-answer tests by taking the quiz below. Circle the correct answer.

1. Which type of test would best measure your knowledge of important names, dates, and events in history?
   a. essay test **b.** short-answer test
2. Which type of test measures your ability to memorize your class notes and the highlights of your reading assignments?
   a. essay test **b.** short-answer test
3. Which type of test would best measure your ability to analyze or compare things?
   a. essay test **b.** short-answer test
4. Which type of test requires you to summarize key points about a topic?
   a. essay test **b.** short-answer test
5. Which type of test usually requires you to complete a sentence correctly?
   a. essay test **b.** short-answer test

52 **Level C** • Achieve Mastery

Rate Yourself

ANSWERS: 1. b, 2. b, 3. a, 4. a, 5. b.

Were all your answers correct? If so, you're well on your way to understanding how to conquer short-answer and essay tests. Read on to develop more test-taking strategies. If these types of tests are still a mystery to you, don't panic. This lesson will help you get on the right track.

How to Tackle Tests

What strategies do you use to study for essay and short-answer tests? Do you vary your study method when you know these types of questions will be on the tests?

Get together in a small group and discuss ways that each of you study differently for various tests. List your ideas below.

Study Strategies for Short-Answer Tests

Study Strategies for Essay Tests

Plan an Essay

Did you know that the French word *essay* means "to try or attempt"? Read the four essay questions below. Give your best effort to plan an answer for one of the essay questions. Use the space to make a brief web or outline that shows what you would write.

1. *Summarize the roles of the three branches of the U.S. government: executive, legislative, and judicial.*
2. *Compare and contrast the Vietnam War and the Persian Gulf War.*
3. *Describe the way an invention you use every day works.*
4. *Explain the term interdependence as it relates to Earth's living things.*

Share your outline or web with a partner. Discuss similarities and differences and talk about how you would use your plans to write complete essays.

Unit 5 • Developing Test-Taking Skills 53

Pages 54–55

- **Short-Answer Questions**
  Discuss the tips and invite students to add others. If necessary, review singular and plural verbs and demonstrate how to write answers in the correct form.
- **Story Problems**
  Students can practice handling story problems by reading examples from a math textbook and pointing out the question and the relevant information.
- **Essay Questions**
  Rewriting the question as a topic sentence is a good way for students to begin an essay answer in a focused, organized way. Ask students to practice this technique using the essay questions from page 53.
- **Where Are You Going?**
  Ask students to write a goal that will help them improve their performance on short-answer and essay tests.

Teacher Modeling

You may wish to use or adapt these examples of teacher modeling.

To answer a short-answer question:

- I reread the question to make sure I understand it.
- I look for context clues.
- I check to see if *a* or *an* comes before the blank and if the verb is singular or plural.

To solve a story problem:

- I study the problem to see what information is relevant.
- I figure out what process to use and what form my final answer should take.

To answer an essay question:

- I turn the question into a topic sentence.
- I outline what I plan to write.
- I plan my time carefully.

Tips for Answering Short-Answer and Essay Questions

Short-Answer Questions

To complete a short-answer test, you usually fill in blanks in incomplete sentences. You're not given any answers to choose from, so you need to generate the answer, or "pull it out of your mind." That means you have to have studied hard enough to have the answer in your mind in the first place!

The purpose of short-answer questions is to test your recall of key terms, facts, and details. If you memorize your class notes and the highlights of your reading assignments, you should have no problem recalling the answers to short-answer questions. Just in case you run into trouble, though, here are a few tips that may help:

- Reread the question several times.
- Watch for context clues in the question or in other questions on the test.
- Check to see if the word before the blank is *a* or *an*. If it's *an*, the correct answer begins with a vowel.
- Check the verb in the sentence. If it's singular, the answer must be singular. If it's plural, the answer must be plural.
- Answer the easy questions first. Then go back to the harder questions. The answers to some questions may help you recall the answers to others.

Story Problems

Story problems are a special kind of short-answer question. You'll often find them on math and science tests. To answer a story problem, you read a passage, analyze it to find the question or problem, determine the appropriate method for solving it, apply the method correctly, and express the answer in the correct form. If you're having difficulty with a story problem, ask yourself these questions:

- What exactly is the problem or question?
- What information is provided? Will I use all of it to answer the question?
- Can I make a diagram or picture to help me solve the problem?
- How have I answered similar questions in the past?
- What form should my answer take?

These questions will help you locate information in the story problem. Find the clues, write them down, translate them into symbols and sentences, and study them closely. Soon you will see the key to the problem. As you work out the problem, show all your steps and calculations clearly. Even if your answer is wrong, you may get partial credit if the method you used is correct.

Build your test-taking confidence by trying these tips.

54 **Level C** • Achieve Mastery

Essay Questions

Essay answers may range from a few sentences to a few paragraphs in length. Your essay answer should be as carefully worded and well organized as a full-length essay or report. Use these strategies to write clear, thoughtful essay answers in a short amount of time:

- **Plan your time carefully.** It's easy to forget about time when you become engrossed in answering an essay question, but don't! Watch the clock and pace yourself accordingly. Be sure to allow time to answer all the questions on the test.
- **Know your facts.** Make sure you've prepared for the test thoroughly. That way you can concentrate on your writing rather than trying to think of something to say.
- **Start with an outline or web.** As with other writing assignments, start with a brief outline. Your outline will help you write your thoughts in logical order. And if you run out of time before you finish your answer, the outline or web will show your teacher where you were headed.
- **Write legibly.** Obviously, if your teacher can't read what you've written it won't count for much!
- **Use complete sentences.** Don't let the time limit rattle you. Write full sentences just as you ordinarily would. Use transition words, such as *first*, *second*, and *finally*, that clearly demonstrate how one thought logically follows another.
- **Rewrite the question in the form of a statement** and announce what you're going to write about in your opening paragraph. Use the main body of your answer to make your point. End your essay with a concluding paragraph that summarizes your main ideas.

Where Are You Going?

Summarize what you learned in this lesson. ______________________

____

____

____

Now use your summary to write a ***Take Charge!*** goal that will help you become a better student.

____

____

____

Unit 5 • Developing Test-Taking Skills 55

Taking Multiple-Choice Tests

About Multiple-Choice Tests

Most teachers use multiple-choice tests as an assessment tool, and most standardized tests include multiple-choice questions. Because students encounter multiple-choice questions so often, it's important that they know the best strategies for answering them. The purpose of this lesson is to teach students specific strategies for answering multiple-choice questions. The goal is to help students feel at ease with multiple-choice tests so that they will be able to show how much they really know.

Pages 56–57

- **Choices, Choices…**
  Read the introduction with students. Invite students to raise their hands to show whether they chose answer *a, b,* or *c*. Ask volunteers to explain their feelings by relating their experiences with multiple-choice tests.

- **Where Do You Stand?/Rate Yourself**
  After students complete the quiz, check the answers together and read the explanations. Share some strategies you've used when taking multiple-choice tests (see *Teacher Modeling*).

- **Educated Guesses**
  Two of the answers contain the word *soldiers,* so students will properly assume that one is likely to be correct. Since the question mentions that the horse was a *Trojan* horse, students may conclude that the soldiers inside were probably Trojan. The answer, however, is *Greek soldiers*. Only study leads to a truly educated guess.

- **Tricky Tests**
  Ask students to decide on the correct answers: *1) c, 2) d.* Discuss why Jake and Rachel were misled and how they could improve their test-taking skills. Guide students to understand the importance of taking time to read test questions carefully.

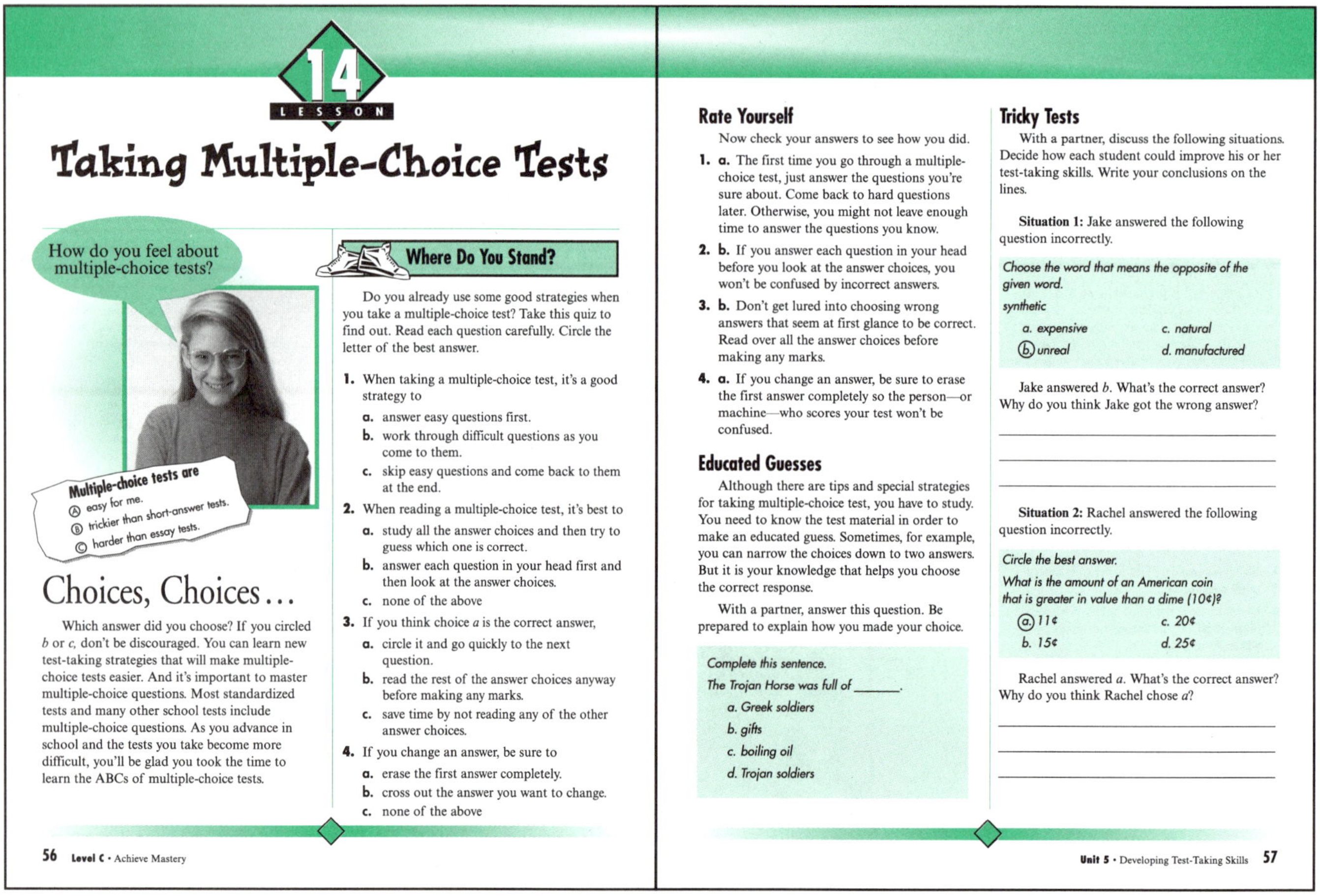

14
LESSON

Taking Multiple-Choice Tests

How do you feel about multiple-choice tests?

Multiple-choice tests are
Ⓐ easy for me.
Ⓑ trickier than short-answer tests.
Ⓒ harder than essay tests.

Choices, Choices…

Which answer did you choose? If you circled *b* or *c,* don't be discouraged. You can learn new test-taking strategies that will make multiple-choice tests easier. And it's important to master multiple-choice questions. Most standardized tests and many other school tests include multiple-choice questions. As you advance in school and the tests you take become more difficult, you'll be glad you took the time to learn the ABCs of multiple-choice tests.

Where Do You Stand?

Do you already use some good strategies when you take a multiple-choice test? Take this quiz to find out. Read each question carefully. Circle the letter of the best answer.

1. When taking a multiple-choice test, it's a good strategy to
   a. answer easy questions first.
   b. work through difficult questions as you come to them.
   c. skip easy questions and come back to them at the end.
2. When reading a multiple-choice test, it's best to
   a. study all the answer choices and then try to guess which one is correct.
   b. answer each question in your head first and then look at the answer choices.
   c. none of the above
3. If you think choice *a* is the correct answer,
   a. circle it and go quickly to the next question.
   b. read the rest of the answer choices anyway before making any marks.
   c. save time by not reading any of the other answer choices.
4. If you change an answer, be sure to
   a. erase the first answer completely.
   b. cross out the answer you want to change.
   c. none of the above

56 Level C • Achieve Mastery

Rate Yourself

Now check your answers to see how you did.

1. a. The first time you go through a multiple-choice test, just answer the questions you're sure about. Come back to hard questions later. Otherwise, you might not leave enough time to answer the questions you know.
2. b. If you answer each question in your head before you look at the answer choices, you won't be confused by incorrect answers.
3. b. Don't get lured into choosing wrong answers that seem at first glance to be correct. Read over all the answer choices before making any marks.
4. a. If you change an answer, be sure to erase the first answer completely so the person—or machine—who scores your test won't be confused.

Educated Guesses

Although there are tips and special strategies for taking multiple-choice test, you have to study. You need to know the test material in order to make an educated guess. Sometimes, for example, you can narrow the choices down to two answers. But it is your knowledge that helps you choose the correct response.

With a partner, answer this question. Be prepared to explain how you made your choice.

Complete this sentence.
The Trojan Horse was full of ______.
a. Greek soldiers
b. gifts
c. boiling oil
d. Trojan soldiers

Tricky Tests

With a partner, discuss the following situations. Decide how each student could improve his or her test-taking skills. Write your conclusions on the lines.

Situation 1: Jake answered the following question incorrectly.

Choose the word that means the opposite of the given word.
synthetic
a. expensive *c. natural*
ⓑ unreal *d. manufactured*

Jake answered *b*. What's the correct answer? Why do you think Jake got the wrong answer?

____

Situation 2: Rachel answered the following question incorrectly.

Circle the best answer.
What is the amount of an American coin that is greater in value than a dime (10¢)?
ⓐ 11¢ *c. 20¢*
b. 15¢ *d. 25¢*

Rachel answered *a*. What's the correct answer? Why do you think Rachel chose *a*?

____

Unit 5 • Developing Test-Taking Skills 57

Pages 58–59

- **Multiple-Choice Tests for Reading**
  Multiple-Choice Tests for Math
  After students read the tips, challenge them to write tips for science tests.
- **Watch Out for Negative Words!**
  Is Anything ALWAYS True?
  Encourage students to name more words that change the meaning of a question or signal that an answer choice may be incorrect.
- **Does Long Equal Correct?**
  Forget About Patterns
  Many students have absorbed test-taking myths from classmates or older siblings. Allow students to discuss the truth behind the myths.
- **DOs and DON'Ts**
  Invite students to add ideas to each list.
- **Where Are You Going?**
  Ask students to write a goal that includes strategies for their next multiple-choice test.

Teacher Modeling

You may wish to use or adapt these examples of teacher modeling.

When I take a multiple-choice test:

- I keep an extra pencil and eraser with me.
- I read the directions and questions carefully.
- I read all choices before I decide on an answer.
- I answer easy questions first.
- If I skip a question, I make sure to skip the number on the answer sheet, too.
- I usually stick with my first answer; I don't change an answer unless I have a good reason for changing it.
- I read questions about a reading passage first, so I know what to look for as I read.
- I use extra time to review my answers.
- I make sure answers I changed are erased completely.

Hints for Taking Multiple-Choice Tests

Multiple-Choice Tests for Reading

- When you answer multiple-choice questions about a reading passage, read the questions before you read the selection. That way, you'll know what to look for as you read the passage.
- Questions about factual details often ask about the *Five Ws—Who, What, When, Where,* and *Why*. You can get a head start if you look for details that answer these questions as you read.
- If you know about the subject of the selection, don't assume that you can answer questions from your prior knowledge. Look back at the selection to find support for your answers.

Multiple-Choice Tests for Math

- Read each question carefully to find out what you need to do. Then reread it to find the specific information you need to solve the problem.
- Before you read the answer choices, estimate what you think the answer will be.
- Work out math problems in the margins, on the back of the test, or on scrap paper. Draw pictures, charts, or tables if they will help you.
- For a measurement or geometry problem, first write down the formula you need to solve the problem. Then plug in the numbers from the problem.

Watch Out for Negative Words!

Be aware of negative words such as *not* or *opposite* in questions or directions. It's easy to skip over these words when you're nervous or in a hurry. If you don't read the question slowly and carefully, you may find yourself choosing the answer that is exactly the opposite of the correct one.

Is Anything ALWAYS True?

Watch out for questions or answer choices that include words such as *all, none, always, never,* and *every*. Very few absolute statements are true in every possible case. If one of the words above appears in a question or answer, think hard. Try to find an exception to the statement.

Does Long Equal Correct?

With multiple-choice responses, the longest, most complicated and carefully written answer may be correct because of the detailed information that is included. This is not an absolute rule, but a general principle to keep in mind. Rereading the longest answer is a good place to start when you're unsure of the correct answer.

Forget About Patterns

Don't even bother to look for a pattern in the answers. Most teachers and test-makers know that students often do this, so they usually check to make sure no pattern exists. They may even try to trick you by making one letter correct more often than others or by using a letter only one or two times—or not at all. Don't expect that you'll be marking the same number of *a*'s, *b*'s, *c*'s, and *d*'s.

58 **Level C** • Achieve Mastery

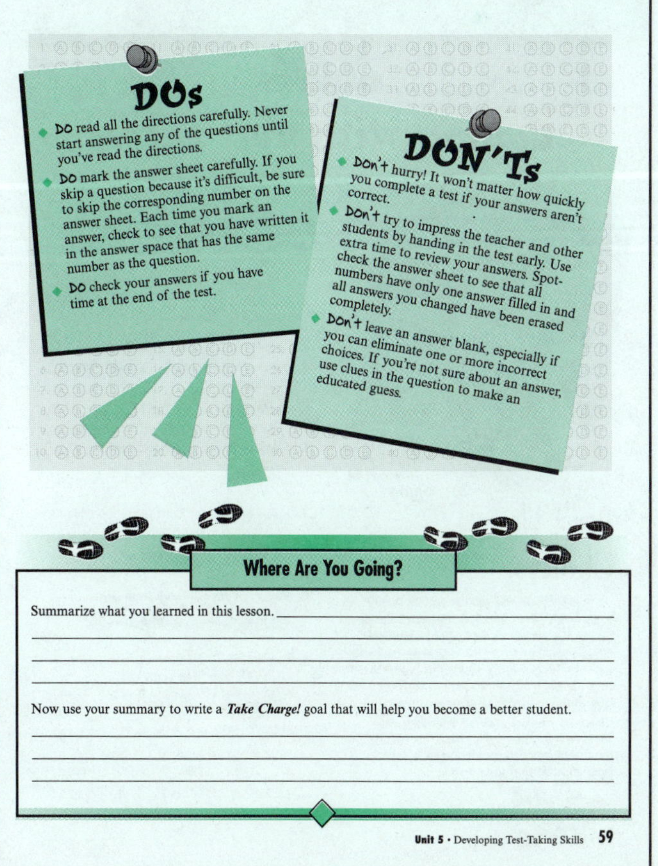

DOs

- DO read all the directions carefully. Never start answering any of the questions until you've read the directions.
- DO mark the answer sheet carefully. If you skip a question because it's difficult, be sure to skip the corresponding number on the answer sheet. Each time you mark an answer, check to see that you have written it in the answer space that has the same number as the question.
- DO check your answers if you have time at the end of the test.

DON'Ts

- Don't hurry! It won't matter how quickly you complete a test if your answers aren't correct.
- Don't try to impress the teacher and other students by handing in the test early. Use extra time to review your answers. Spot-check the answer sheet to see that all numbers have only one answer filled in and all answers you changed have been erased completely.
- Don't leave an answer blank, especially if you can eliminate one or more incorrect choices. If you're not sure about an answer, use clues in the question to make an educated guess.

Where Are You Going?

Summarize what you learned in this lesson. ______

Now use your summary to write a *Take Charge!* goal that will help you become a better student.

Unit 5 • Developing Test-Taking Skills 59

Coping With Test Stress

About Test Stress

Everyone experiences stress at some time in their lives. Students are no exception. It's important for them to realize that anxiety before a big test, an oral report, or an important school event is natural. The purpose of this lesson is to help students learn effective strategies for coping with test stress so that overwhelming anxiety doesn't interfere with their ability to focus and to perform well.

Pages 60–61

◆ **Don't Worry, Be Happy**
After reading the lesson introduction, ask volunteers to share their experiences with test stress. Engage students in a discussion about the physical and mental reactions they've had as a result of stress. Help students understand that some anxiety is normal when they are under pressure, but that there are ways to cope with test stress and reduce its effects.

◆ **Where Do You Stand?/Rate Yourself**
Students can assess what they know about stress by taking the quiz and reading the explanation for each answer.

◆ **Calming Ideas**
Ask students to talk with a partner about methods they've used to cope with stress. Ask students to express their ideas in the form of an acrostic poem like the one pictured. Invite volunteers to read their poems to the class. After students finish, explain some of the strategies you use to cope with stress (see *Teacher Modeling*).

◆ **Challenge Irrational Thoughts**
Many students who experience stress are harder on themselves than on others. Putting themselves in another person's place can help them recognize thoughts that stand in the way of success. Encourage students to write persuasive, upbeat advice. Remind them to reread their arguments in times of stress.

---

15 LESSON

Coping With Test Stress

It's hard not to worry on the day of the BIG TEST.

Don't Worry, Be Happy

Don't Worry, Be Happy is a good title for a song, but it's hard advice for many people to follow. It's natural to worry and feel anxious about important events like big tests. And a little stress isn't a bad thing. Stress can motivate you to work and study harder and to perform your best. But overwhelming anxiety can interfere with your ability to focus. Learning how to reduce anxiety and cope with stress can make important events more comfortable. It can even improve your test scores!

Where Do You Stand?

How much do you already know about coping with test stress? Take the following quiz to find out. Circle *True* or *False* to answer each question.

1. Stress affects you both physically and mentally.
   True False
2. Adrenaline is a stress hormone.
   True False
3. Stress makes your heart pump more blood and decreases your breathing rate.
   True False
4. Sweaty palms can result from stress.
   True False
5. One way to cope with stress is to breathe shallowly from your abdomen.
   True False

60 Level C • Achieve Mastery

Rate Yourself

Check your answers to see how much you know about stress.

1. **True**—Stress can increase your heart rate, raise your blood pressure, and make your muscles tense. It can also slow your thinking process and make you irritable and depressed.
2. **True**—When you're anxious, your nervous system produces stress hormones, including adrenaline.
3. **False**—Stress increases your breathing rate, causing more oxygen to be sent to your larger muscles.
4. **True**—When you're under stress, sweat glands become activated to protect your body from becoming overheated.
5. **False**—One way to relax and cope with stress is to breathe deeply from your abdomen. If you breathe shallowly, you may not get enough oxygen. Taking rapid shallow breaths can lead to hyperventilation.

Calming Ideas

With a partner, brainstorm ways to cope with test stress. Then, using a separate sheet of paper, work together to write an acrostic poem to help you remember some of the methods you discussed. Use one letter of a word like *calm* or *stress* to begin each line of your poem. Share your poems with the class.

Study effectively
Take deep breaths
Relax your muscles
Exercise daily
Sleep eight hours at night
Stay confident

Challenge Irrational Thoughts

If you're a person who experiences test anxiety, some of the irrational thoughts below may sound familiar.

Imagine that a classmate has come to you and voiced these thoughts. On the lines below each statement, write the argument you would use to talk your friend out of the discouraging thought. Share your ideas with the class. Then, the next time you have a similar thought before a test, you can turn back to this page and reread your argument.

1. It doesn't matter how hard I study. I still won't do well on this test.
2. I'm the worst student in my class.
3. What if I'm so nervous I can't remember any of the answers?
4. No matter how hard I study, I'm just not smart enough to do well on this test.
5. I'd rather stay home sick than go to school and take the test.

Unit 5 • Developing Test-Taking Skills 61

Pages 62–63

- **Relax Your Muscles**
  Exercise Your Smile
  Have students read these sections on their own. They describe physical methods for controlling stress. Encourage students to practice the relaxation technique. They can use this method before and during tests to drain tension from their bodies. Ask volunteers to share jokes or mental pictures that make them smile.
- **Avoid Cramming**
  Be Prepared!
  Ask students to read the advice about things they can do ahead of time to prevent stress. Ask the class to brainstorm ways to prepare for tests, including *listening in class, taking notes,* and *scheduling plenty of study time*.
- **Where Are You Going?**
  Ask students to write a goal that will help them cope with test stress in the future.

Teacher Modeling

You may wish to use or adapt these examples of teacher modeling.

When I feel anxious:

- I write about my feelings—putting my worries into words makes them seem more manageable.
- I think about my successes. This helps me stay confident and think positive thoughts.
- I take a break and do something unrelated to the task that's making me anxious.

To calm myself:

- I close my eyes and take deep breaths.
- I focus on tensing and then relaxing the muscles in my face, hands, and other parts of my body.
- I create a mental picture of a peaceful scene, such as a field of wildflowers.
- I think about something funny. That makes me smile to release the tension.

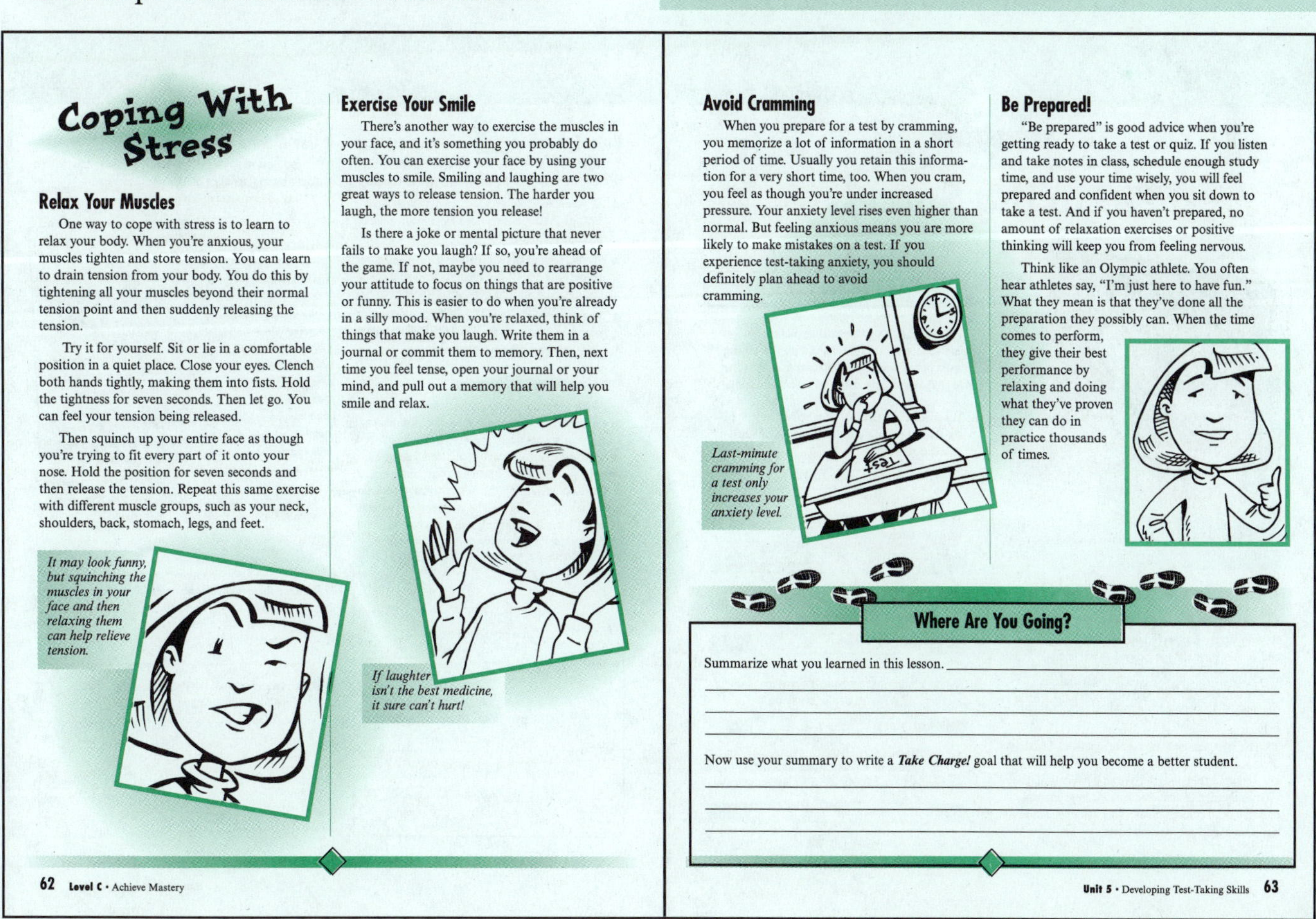

Coping With Stress

Relax Your Muscles

One way to cope with stress is to learn to relax your body. When you're anxious, your muscles tighten and store tension. You can learn to drain tension from your body. You do this by tightening all your muscles beyond their normal tension point and then suddenly releasing the tension.

Try it for yourself. Sit or lie in a comfortable position in a quiet place. Close your eyes. Clench both hands tightly, making them into fists. Hold the tightness for seven seconds. Then let go. You can feel your tension being released.

Then squinch up your entire face as though you're trying to fit every part of it onto your nose. Hold the position for seven seconds and then release the tension. Repeat this same exercise with different muscle groups, such as your neck, shoulders, back, stomach, legs, and feet.

It may look funny, but squinching the muscles in your face and then relaxing them can help relieve tension.

Exercise Your Smile

There's another way to exercise the muscles in your face, and it's something you probably do often. You can exercise your face by using your muscles to smile. Smiling and laughing are two great ways to release tension. The harder you laugh, the more tension you release!

Is there a joke or mental picture that never fails to make you laugh? If so, you're ahead of the game. If not, maybe you need to rearrange your attitude to focus on things that are positive or funny. This is easier to do when you're already in a silly mood. When you're relaxed, think of things that make you laugh. Write them in a journal or commit them to memory. Then, next time you feel tense, open your journal or your mind, and pull out a memory that will help you smile and relax.

If laughter isn't the best medicine, it sure can't hurt!

62 Level C • Achieve Mastery

Avoid Cramming

When you prepare for a test by cramming, you memorize a lot of information in a short period of time. Usually you retain this information for a very short time, too. When you cram, you feel as though you're under increased pressure. Your anxiety level rises even higher than normal. But feeling anxious means you are more likely to make mistakes on a test. If you experience test-taking anxiety, you should definitely plan ahead to avoid cramming.

Last-minute cramming for a test only increases your anxiety level.

Be Prepared!

"Be prepared" is good advice when you're getting ready to take a test or quiz. If you listen and take notes in class, schedule enough study time, and use your time wisely, you will feel prepared and confident when you sit down to take a test. And if you haven't prepared, no amount of relaxation exercises or positive thinking will keep you from feeling nervous.

Think like an Olympic athlete. You often hear athletes say, "I'm just here to have fun." What they mean is that they've done all the preparation they possibly can. When the time comes to perform, they give their best performance by relaxing and doing what they've proven they can do in practice thousands of times.

Where Are You Going?

Summarize what you learned in this lesson. ________________

Now use your summary to write a *Take Charge!* goal that will help you become a better student.

Unit 5 • Developing Test-Taking Skills 63

Picturing Success

About Picturing Success

It's often said that "a picture is worth a thousand words." Young children know the value of pictures, but adolescents and adults are more likely to rely on written words as they read, study, and follow directions. In this lesson, students will learn to form mental pictures and use them to visualize the road to success, to make what they read come alive, and to remember what they learn. By learning and practicing visualization techniques, students will use both their logical left brain and their more intuitive, artistic right brain to become more successful in every way.

Pages 64–65

- **Go for the Gold!**
Encourage students who participate in sports to tell how they use visualization techniques to prepare for and get through a performance. Then ask students to tell how they might use mental pictures to help them with other kinds of tasks. Share some of the ways you use mental pictures (see *Teacher Modeling*).
- **Where Do You Stand?/Rate Yourself**
Students can begin thinking about the role mental pictures already play in their everyday lives by completing the quiz.
- **Practice Mental Pictures**
Ask partners to choose three activities and describe mental pictures they might use to improve their performance. For example, picturing a neat, completed page of math problems may help students finish their homework.
- **Use Mental Pictures**
Tell students to read the story excerpt as quickly as they can and then, without writing their answers yet, try to answer the questions. Then ask them to reread, pausing to form mental pictures. After rereading, they can write their answers. Discuss how making mental pictures helped them remember details.

16 LESSON

Picturing Success

What is this gymnast thinking?

Go for the Gold!

Do you think the gymnast is picturing herself staying firmly on the balance beam through the end of her routine? Or do you think she's picturing herself falling to the ground with a big thump? If she's picturing success, she's likely to succeed. If she's picturing a fall, it will probably happen.

The best athletes use mental pictures to boost their scores. Before they perform, they picture exactly what they will do. While performing, they picture themselves succeeding. Making mental pictures is an important skill for athletes. It's an important skill for students, too.

Where Do You Stand?

How well do you use mental pictures to get yourself through your day? Find out by taking the quiz below. Read the statements. Fill in the circle that shows how often you do each thing.

1. When I'm worried about whether or not I'll be able to do something, I picture myself succeeding.
Hardly Ever ① ② ③ ④ ⑤ Almost Always
2. When I read directions, I picture myself going through each step.
Hardly Ever ① ② ③ ④ ⑤ Almost Always
3. Before I begin a new project, I imagine what the end product will look like.
Hardly Ever ① ② ③ ④ ⑤ Almost Always
4. When I listen to someone, I form mental pictures of what he or she is saying.
Hardly Ever ① ② ③ ④ ⑤ Almost Always
5. When I think of a place, such as a forest or a seashore, I can clearly see it in my mind's eye.
Hardly Ever ① ② ③ ④ ⑤ Almost Always

64 **Level C** • Achieve Mastery

Rate Yourself

To rate your skills, add up the numbers in the circles you filled in. Write your total in the box.

- If you scored 20 or more, congratulations! You probably understand the importance of mental pictures.
- If you scored between 15 and 19, you know something about the technique. Using it consistently should help you succeed.
- If you scored below 15, try forming mental pictures. You may see a rapid improvement in your schoolwork and your attitude.

Practice Mental Pictures

With a partner, talk about activities you want to succeed in, such as taking a test, performing in a music or sports event, or mastering a new type of math problem. Describe pictures you could hold in your mind to improve your performance in these activities. On the chart below, list three of the activities. Then write descriptions of the mental pictures you think will help you succeed.

Activity	Mental Picture

Use Mental Pictures

As you read the story excerpt below, try to form mental images of the characters and setting. Then answer the questions.

I waited for Lori at the playground where we agreed to meet. It was weird, because she and I spent a lot of time here, once. I thought of her on a cold day at recess, jacket unzipped, hair flying. She ran with ease in a complicated path around the yard. Like a bee hovering over flowers, she stopped to ask one group of kids to join a game, to tell another group some dumb kid joke, or to lobby the teacher on recess duty for five more minutes of play time. Lori never walked. She needed me to help her, though. I helped her with math, and with her family, which was a little on the mixed-up side. That was years ago, two years since I had even talked to her. But today I needed her help. Boy, did I need help. The playground was empty, desolate. When would she get here?

1. Describe the most vivid mental picture you were able to form.
2. List three words that describe your mental picture of the playground.
3. In the space below, draw a picture that illustrates the story.

Unit 6 • Participating in Class 65

Pages 66–67

◆ **Hold On to Your Talent**
Give Yourself 20/20 Inner Vision
Ask students to read these sections on their own. They provide a rationale for using mental pictures and describe a way to develop visualizing skills. To practice, ask students to picture a familiar place, such as the cafeteria. Encourage students to close their eyes, recall as many details as they can, and describe what they see. List details they recall on the board.

◆ **Listening With Pictures**
Step-by-Step Directions
These sections explain ways students can put mental pictures to work in class. You may want to read aloud a few paragraphs from a social studies text so students can practice using visualization to be active listeners.

◆ **Where Are You Going?**
Ask students to write a goal for using mental pictures to improve academic performance.

Teacher Modeling

You may wish to use or adapt these examples of teacher modeling.

To use mental pictures to boost my performance:

- I picture myself going through each step of the activity.
- I picture myself succeeding.

To use mental pictures to follow directions:

- I picture what I want my end product to look like.
- I read the directions and picture myself completing each step.

To use mental pictures to be a more active listener:

- I listen for adjectives that describe how things look.
- I imagine that I'm part of the scene I'm picturing.

All About Mental Pictures

Hold On to Your Talent

When you were a young child, you probably formed mental pictures all the time without realizing it. All human beings are born with the ability to visualize, and most people keep that ability through their early teen years. But almost half of all adults in our culture lose the ability to form mental pictures—they simply forget how. This happens in spite of the fact that our culture places a high value on creativity, imagination, and intuition—all of which are based on the ability to form mental pictures.

Forming mental pictures adds interest to the things you read and hear. Your mental pictures will make faraway places and long ago events seem more real to you. The fact is that visualization is an extremely important learning tool. Mental pictures can help you remember important details and solve complex problems. Are you still able to form mental pictures easily? Remember that visualizing is a special talent. Read on to find out how you can hold on to your visualizing skills—and make them even better.

Give Yourself 20/20 Inner Vision

Some people who grew up before television was invented will tell you that listening to radio was more fun than watching television is today. That, they say, is because they had to make up pictures to go along with the stories they heard, and their mental pictures were usually better than the real thing. These same people may no longer have the ability to visualize. They don't have to visualize anymore, since television provides all the pictures they need. Without practice, they lost some of their talent.

You don't need to give up television to develop your talent for making mental pictures. Visualization is a skill that can be improved with practice. Here's a simple way to begin improving your visualization skills. Find a quiet spot where you can get comfortable and relax. Close your eyes, take a few deep breaths. Then tell yourself to picture a circle. Wait a few moments, and a circle should come floating into "view." Keep practicing with simple shapes like circles, squares, and triangles. Then move on to more complicated images—street scenes, a view from the top of a mountain, or the sun setting over the ocean. At first, picture familiar places. Then move on to imaginary scenes. Keep practicing. Soon your mental pictures will be as good as the ones you see on TV.

Do you form a mental picture in your mind of succeeding before beginning a task?

66 Level C • Achieve Mastery

Listening With Pictures

The next time you're listening in class, try adding your own mental pictures. As your teacher speaks, try picturing what he or she is saying in your mind's eye. If the subject is a Civil War battle, for example, put yourself in the thick of the action. See the smoke from the gun barrels, hear the roar of the cannons. If the subject is how plants get nutrients from the soil, visualize water from the soil carrying nutrients into the plant's roots and up its stem to the leaves. But make sure you know the difference between visualizing and daydreaming. The helpful kind of visualizing is all about listening closely and actively to what the speaker has to say. It helps you remember what you hear.

Step-by-Step Directions

Making mental pictures can help you follow directions, too. Whether you're building a model, working on a project, writing a research report, or just doing your homework, mentally rehearsing the steps can help you get it right the first time. As you read the directions, imagine yourself going through every step. If you come to a point where you're not sure what to do next, or if you think you've done something wrong, reread the directions and retrace your steps. When you've pictured yourself walking through all the steps and completing the project perfectly, you're ready to begin the project for real.

Where Are You Going?

Summarize what you learned in this lesson. ____________________

Now use your summary to write a ***Take Charge!*** goal that will help you become a better student.

____

Unit 6 • Participating in Class 67

Asking and Answering Questions

About Questions

Many students feel insecure or uncertain about asking questions. Their self-consciousness often keeps them from finding out things they need to know. In this lesson, students will learn the etiquette of asking and answering questions. More importantly, they'll learn that questions are their best tools for being an active reader and listener.

Pages 68–69

- **A Cliché That's True**
As you read the introduction with your class, ask students to answer the questions in the second paragraph with a show of hands. Most will probably indicate that they sometimes avoid asking questions for fear of what others will think. Knowing they are not alone in their fears is the first step toward abandoning self-consciousness. Explain some of your own strategies for asking and answering questions (see *Teacher Modeling*).

- **Where Do You Stand?/Rate Yourself**
Ask students to take the quiz and evaluate their responses with a partner. In a follow-up discussion, ask pairs to share their conclusions. Discuss appropriate ways for students to ask and answer questions in the classroom.

- **Questions for Clarity**
In this activity, students gain experience in asking precise questions and giving informative answers. Afterward, partners can use the discussion questions to analyze their questioning techniques.

- **Use Your Curiosity**
Students will learn to become more active readers as they generate questions about newspaper headlines. Ask volunteers to share their questions with the class. For *Cause of Air Crash Found,* students might ask *What was the cause of the air crash?, How was the cause of the air crash found?,* etc. Encourage students to practice the strategy at home by making up questions about TV shows.

Asking and Answering Questions

A Cliché That's True

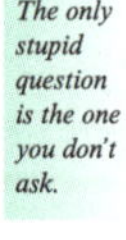

The only stupid question is the one you don't ask.

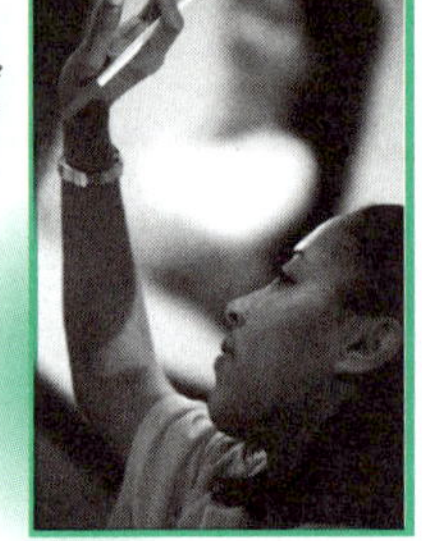

No one knows who originated this often-heard cliché. Chances are it was a teacher. Clichés are phrases you should usually avoid—they're tired, overused expressions. But the strange thing about clichés is that they can be true.

Have you ever avoided asking a question because you thought everyone else knew the answer? Have you ever been afraid people would think your question was "dumb"? If so, you've probably learned the hard way that "the only stupid question is the one you don't ask."

Where Do You Stand?

See where you stand on the question of questions. Circle the letter of the answer that best expresses how you usually respond.

1. If you think of a question while your teacher is speaking, you usually
   a. go ahead and say it right out loud.
   b. raise your hand and wait to be called on.
   c. jot down your question and ask it after your teacher has finished.
   d. say nothing and hope someone else asks your question.
2. If your teacher asks you a question and you don't know the answer, you usually
   a. say nothing.
   b. make something up.
   c. admit that you don't know.
   d. pretend you didn't hear.
3. If you don't understand the answer to a question, you usually
   a. pretend that you do.
   b. ask for clarification.
   c. look it up in the encyclopedia.
   d. nod your head wisely.
4. If you have a question about something you're reading, you usually
   a. read the section again.
   b. check in another book.
   c. discuss it with your teacher.
   d. hope that it isn't very important.

68 Level C • Achieve Mastery

Rate Yourself

Discuss your answers with a partner. Decide together which response would work best for each situation. Then reread the choices you did not choose and explain why they are not the best course of action.

Questions for Clarity

In Lesson 16, you learned about the importance of being able to form mental pictures. In this activity, you will work with a partner to combine your skill in questioning with your ability to form clear mental pictures.

You and your partner will take turns describing a particular place. You might describe your room, a museum, a park, a festival, a farm, or a place you visited while on vacation. Once you have completed your description, your partner will ask you all the questions he or she needs to be able to create a clear mental picture of the place you have described. Then switch roles. Your partner will give a description, and you get to ask the questions.

Finally, discuss these questions about the questions you asked each other.

- Did you ask many questions that required simple *yes* or *no* answers?
- Did you ask open-ended questions, ones that required longer answers?
- Did you have to rephrase any questions?
- How did your questions help you create better mental pictures?

Use Your Curiosity

Most people don't read every word in a newspaper. They use the headlines to decide which stories to read. If the headline gives you all the information you need, you may not need to read the whole article. But if the headline raises more questions in your mind, you'll probably read on to answer your questions. A headline like *Home team loses on fumble* may tell a casual sports fan everything he or she wants to know: Our team lost. For other readers, the headline may raise questions such as these: Who made the fumble? Was it a close, exciting game? What did the coach have to say about it? What did the player who fumbled have to say? For these readers, their questions have aroused their curiosity.

Read each newspaper headline. Make up a question for each headline. Then draw a star beside the headline whose story you'd most like to read.

1. Cause of Air Crash Found
2. Vegetables Can Be Bad for You
3. Teen Drug Use Is Down
4. New Safety Device Prevents Car Accidents
5. Cure Found for Deadly Disease

Unit 6 • Participating in Class 69

Pages 70–71

- **Asking and Answering Questions**
  Ask a volunteer to read each section aloud. Invite students to recall times they have used any of the tips and to share good and bad experiences related to asking and answering questions. Finally, ask volunteers to describe strategies they've used to overcome their fears of speaking up in class.
- **The Best Time to Ask**
  You may wish to provide a textbook passage or class handout for use with this activity. After groups have tried the three techniques and discussed the results, ask them to report their findings to the class. Did groups find that speakers had different preferences than questioners?
- **Where Are You Going?**
  Ask students to write a goal to help them ask and answer questions effectively in the future.

Teacher Modeling

You may wish to use or adapt these examples of teacher modeling.

I ask questions because:

- I need to find out specific information.
- I want to clarify an idea.
- I don't understand directions.
- I find that thinking of and asking questions keeps me involved as I read or listen.

When I have a question I want to ask:

- I wait until the speaker has finished speaking.
- I think before I speak.
- I don't worry about appearing foolish.

When I answer a question:

- I express myself clearly.
- I am polite and courteous so I won't discourage my listeners from asking more questions.

Asking and Answering Questions

Tips for Better Questions and Answers

- Choose an appropriate time to ask your question. Does the speaker encourage questions during the presentation? Should you save your questions until the end?
- If you must save your question until the end of the presentation, jot it down. If the question is answered later in the speech, cross out the question and make a note of the answer.
- Think before you speak. Use simple, straightforward language.
- Set the stage. Tie in your question with something the speaker said. You may want to begin with: *You told us that . . . ,* or *Does this mean . . . ?*
- Listen carefully to the answer. If the answer raises a new question in your mind, ask that question, too.
- If the speaker doesn't understand your question or doesn't give the answer you need, rephrase your question.
- Be polite and courteous. Don't interrupt while the speaker is answering your question.
- Don't be afraid of appearing foolish. If you have a question, someone else probably has the same question. Other listeners will be glad you asked.
- Don't get so involved with your own question that you forget to listen to the questions of others. The answers to their questions will help you, too.

Conquering Your Fears

Many students are timid when it comes to asking and answering questions in class. Often, they feel intimidated for fear of asking a question that others might ridicule. Does this sometimes happen to you?

If it does, don't feel bad. It is a fear you can overcome. Start slowly by answering your teacher's questions when you're sure you know the answer. Get used to hearing yourself speak confidently. Gradually start asking your own questions. Soon you'll find you enjoy being a more active, involved member of the class!

Get Involved

Asking and answering questions during class does a lot more for you than simply clarifying things you don't understand. It also transforms you into an active listener and a more attentive student. If you're paying close enough attention to realize that there are things you don't understand, you're apt to be more focused and alert. And that means you're getting the most out of the time you spend in class.

70 Level C • Achieve Mastery

Question Yourself

When you're reading, create your own questions by turning chapter heads and subheads into questions using the words *Who, What, When, Where, Why,* and *How*. By making up your own questions, you've set your own goals and purposes for reading. You've given yourself a reason to dig in and read.

But what happens if you can't answer your questions when you're working independently? Jot your questions down or mark them with sticky notes. Later you can discuss your questions with your teacher or a study partner.

The Best Time to Ask

Here's a project you can try with some classmates to find the best system for asking and answering questions. Form a small group and assign one person to be the speaker. Find a textbook or a class handout to use. Then try three different questioning strategies. The speaker should read a different textbook selection each time. Each selection should be two or three paragraphs long. Follow these steps:

1. For the first trial, listeners will simply call out any questions that come to mind as the speaker reads.
2. For the second trial, ask the listeners to raise their hands when they have a question. The speaker must acknowledge raised hands as soon as he or she comes to a good stopping point.
3. For the third trial, tell listeners to jot down their questions on a piece of paper and ask them when the speaker is done reading.

When you're finished, discuss as a group which system seemed to work the best. Name different situations in which each method might work best.

Where Are You Going?

Summarize what you learned in this lesson. ______________________

____

Now use your summary to write a ***Take Charge!*** goal that will help you become a better student.

____

Unit 6 • Participating in Class 71

Making Your Vocabulary Grow

About Vocabulary

School-based vocabulary study is an indispensable part of the curriculum. Yet for many students, vocabulary development begins and ends in school. Students learn the specialized words they need to succeed in specific subjects, but they often lack a working vocabulary they can use to make their everyday speech colorful and precise. Students who develop a love of words will naturally want to learn more. But instilling a love of words in students is not enough. Students need skills in vocabulary development. This lesson provides strategies that will help students build their own working vocabularies independently.

Pages 72–73

- **Words, Words, Words!**
  Many middle school students enjoy collecting things like key chains or stuffed animals. After students read the lesson introduction, suggest that they also consider collecting words. Because a word collection is stored in memory, it can never be lost or broken. And unlike many collections, a well-developed vocabulary can be used and enjoyed for a lifetime.
- **Where Do You Stand?**
  Encourage students to focus on habits that help them build vocabulary as they take the quiz. Invite volunteers to name more activities that can help them build their vocabulary automatically. Share some of your own strategies for expanding your personal vocabulary collection (see *Teacher Modeling*).
- **Have Fun With Words**
  Help students discover that vocabulary building can be fun as they create and solve word puzzles. Discuss each type of puzzle with students. If possible, show examples from newspapers or puzzle books. You may want to duplicate some of students' best puzzles so the whole class can enjoy them.

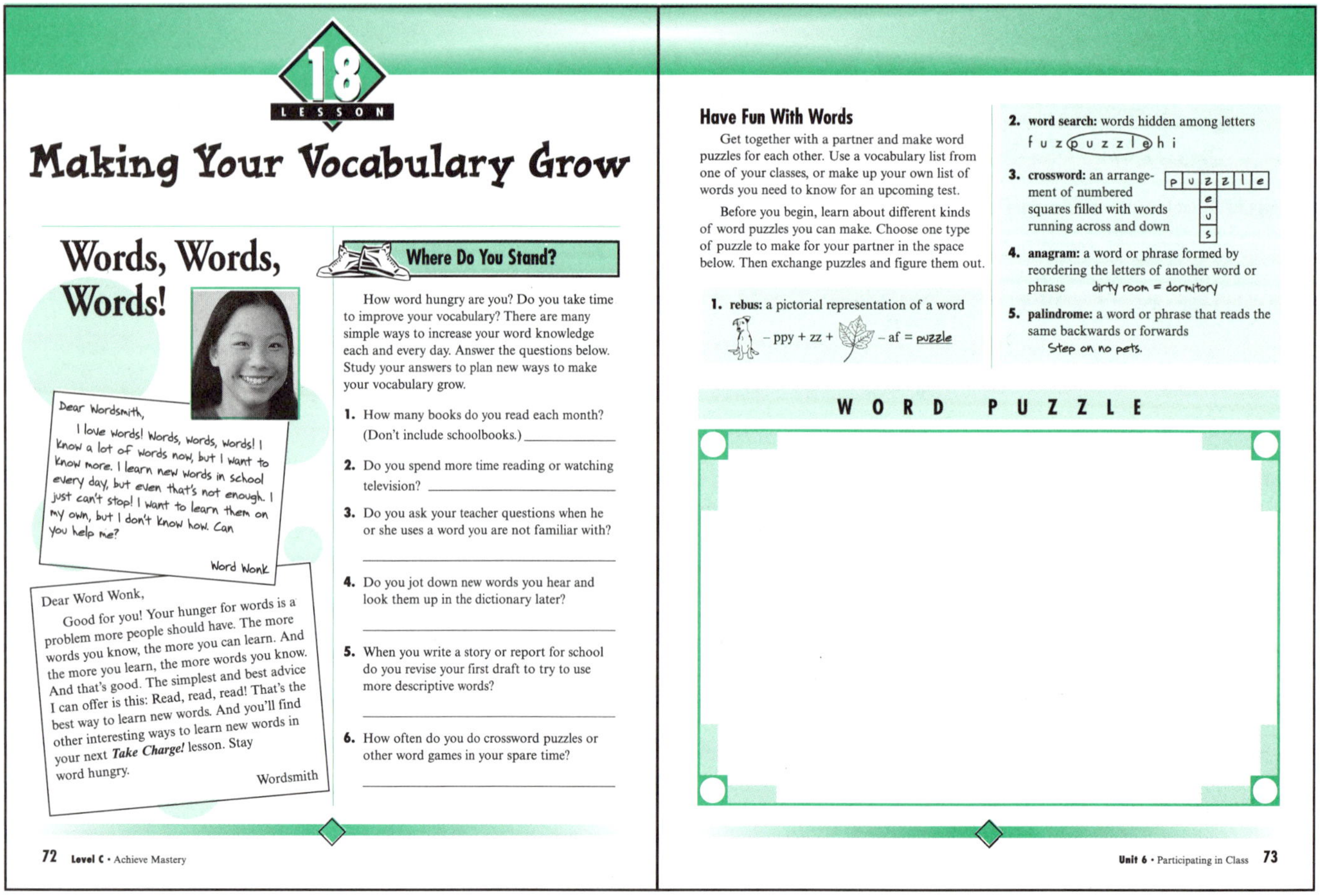

---

18 LESSON

Making Your Vocabulary Grow

Words, Words, Words!

Dear Wordsmith,

I love words! Words, words, words! I know a lot of words now, but I want to know more. I learn new words in school every day, but even that's not enough. I just can't stop! I want to learn them on my own, but I don't know how. Can you help me?

Word Wonk

Dear Word Wonk,

Good for you! Your hunger for words is a problem more people should have. The more words you know, the more you can learn. And the more you learn, the more words you know. And that's good. The simplest and best advice I can offer is this: Read, read, read! That's the best way to learn new words. And you'll find other interesting ways to learn new words in your next *Take Charge!* lesson. Stay word hungry.

Wordsmith

Where Do You Stand?

How word hungry are you? Do you take time to improve your vocabulary? There are many simple ways to increase your word knowledge each and every day. Answer the questions below. Study your answers to plan new ways to make your vocabulary grow.

1. How many books do you read each month? (Don't include schoolbooks.) ______
2. Do you spend more time reading or watching television? ______
3. Do you ask your teacher questions when he or she uses a word you are not familiar with? ______
4. Do you jot down new words you hear and look them up in the dictionary later? ______
5. When you write a story or report for school do you revise your first draft to try to use more descriptive words? ______
6. How often do you do crossword puzzles or other word games in your spare time? ______

72 Level C • Achieve Mastery

Have Fun With Words

Get together with a partner and make word puzzles for each other. Use a vocabulary list from one of your classes, or make up your own list of words you need to know for an upcoming test.

Before you begin, learn about different kinds of word puzzles you can make. Choose one type of puzzle to make for your partner in the space below. Then exchange puzzles and figure them out.

1. **rebus:** a pictorial representation of a word
   [pup] – ppy + zz + [leaf] – af = puzzle
2. **word search:** words hidden among letters
   f u z p u z z l e h i
3. **crossword:** an arrangement of numbered squares filled with words running across and down
   p u z z l e / e u s
4. **anagram:** a word or phrase formed by reordering the letters of another word or phrase
   dirty room = dormitory
5. **palindrome:** a word or phrase that reads the same backwards or forwards
   Step on no pets.

W O R D P U Z Z L E

Unit 6 • Participating in Class 73

Ask which puzzles students found most challenging to solve and which were the most fun to create.

Pages 74–75

- **Make Your Vocabulary Grow!** Ask a volunteer to read each vocabulary-building idea aloud. Suggest that students try one or both self-collection projects by making a personal word card collection or creating a word-a-day calendar. Your class may also enjoy playing a game based on the ideas in *Use Context Clues*. Students begin by writing a sentence made up of simple, familiar words. Then they use a thesaurus to find an obscure synonym for one word. Students can read their sentences aloud, write the difficult word on the board, and challenge the class to guess its meaning from context.
- **Where Are You Going?** Ask students to write a goal that includes strategies for building vocabulary.

Teacher Modeling

You may wish to use or adapt these examples of teacher modeling.

When I encounter an unfamiliar word as I read:

- I skip over it and keep reading to see if the rest of the paragraph will help me understand the meaning.
- I break the word into parts and try to relate the parts to words I know.
- I look it up if I need to.

To build my vocabulary:

- I find ways to use new words in conversation as soon as I learn them.
- I write new words down to help me remember them.
- I read everything I can, from novels and newspapers to signs and cereal boxes.
- I relax by doing crossword puzzles and playing other kinds of word games.

Make Your Vocabulary GROW!

Build Your Word Collection

Collecting words from the world around you can be a hobby like collecting shells on a beach. Your vocabulary collection will be unique. You can share and trade words with other word lovers. The best way to make your word collection grow is to read everything you can get your hands on, from cereal boxes to encyclopedias. You can also collect words you learn in class, words you hear in conversations, and words you hear or see on television.

Write your new words on note cards. Put a rubber band around the cards or place them in a file box or large envelope. Organize your words in alphabetical order. Each time you add new words to your collection, review all the words. Try to use one or two of your words each day.

Use Context Clues

You probably won't need to look up every new word you come across. Often you can use context clues to figure out the meaning of an unfamiliar word. Writers in different subject areas tend to provide different kinds of context clues to help you figure out new words. In science, you might find complete definitions of new words built right into the text. Look at this example:

The ecosystem, a specific situation in which a group of living organisms interact with their environment, is the basic unit of ecology.

It shouldn't be too tough for you to figure out what an *ecosystem* is.

In social studies, writers may provide synonyms to help, like this:

The fibers were spun into yarn, then tied into hanks, or coils, and set aside to be woven.

As you can see, a *hank* is a coil. The more practice you get using context to discover word meanings, the easier it will become.

Recognize Word Structure

Study prefixes, suffixes, and roots. You can often figure out the meanings of new words by breaking them down into parts. Look at the word *geology*. If you know that the root *geo* has something to do with the earth, and that the suffix *logy* means "study of," then you can guess that *geology* means "the study of the earth." If you look up the word *geology* in a dictionary, here's what you'll find: "The scientific study of the origin, history, and structure of the earth." That's pretty close!

74 Level C • Achieve Mastery

Don't Count the Dictionary Out

Even though context clues can often help you understand unfamiliar words, vocabulary reference books are still important tools. Make the dictionary and thesaurus your best friends. Know how to use them and what kinds of information they include. Keep these books at your side as you read, and don't be shy about interrupting your reading to look up a word if you don't understand it from context. Reading on when you don't understand a word is a real waste of time.

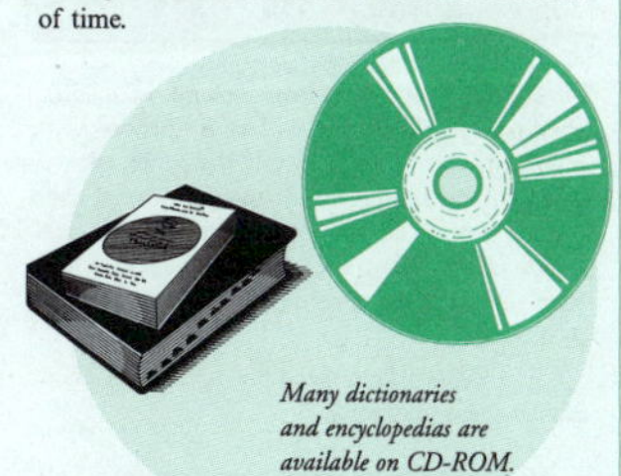

Many dictionaries and encyclopedias are available on CD-ROM.

Do-It-Yourself Vocabulary List

Here's a long-term project that can help your vocabulary grow every single day! Create a word-a-day vocabulary calendar. You can use blank calendar pages. Or you can make a list of dates with space to write a word, its pronunciation, and its definition beside each one.

You can search for interesting words by looking through a dictionary or thesaurus. But the easiest way to find words for your calendar is just to keep your eyes and ears open. Whenever you read or hear an interesting but unfamiliar word, write it in the next open date in your calendar. Then look up the word to find its correct pronunciation and definition.

Check your calendar every morning. Say the word and its definition three times. Make a game of trying to sneak the word into your conversation or writing at least three times during the day. Once a week, review the new words you've learned.

Where Are You Going?

Summarize what you learned in this lesson. ______________________

____

____

____

Now use your summary to write a ***Take Charge!*** goal that will help you become a better student.

____

____

____

Unit 6 • Participating in Class 75

Taking Paraphrased Notes

About Paraphrasing

As middle-school students take more responsibility for their own learning, they rely more and more on note-taking. For some, the challenge of keeping up with the rapid pace of an oral presentation is overwhelming. Students often make the mistake of trying to write down everything the speaker says. Not only is this futile, but students who attempt it usually get caught up in details and miss the main ideas. In this lesson, students will learn how to paraphrase as they take notes on the most important parts of a presentation or reading selection.

Pages 76–77

- **In Other Words. . .**
  Where Do You Stand?/Rate Yourself
  Read the introduction aloud. Guide students to define *paraphrasing* as restating main ideas in one's own words. Then allow time for students to perform the experiment described in *Where Do You Stand?* As you discuss the results, share your own strategies for taking paraphrased notes (see *Teacher Modeling*).

- **Practice Oral Paraphrasing**
  After students have practiced paraphrasing with a partner, ask volunteers to copy their written paraphrased notes on the board. Compare the paraphrases with the original selections, checking to make sure the paraphrased notes include all the main ideas.

- **Familiar Ideas, Unfamiliar Words**
  Most of the proverbs will probably be familiar to most students. If necessary, give the answers: *1) Too many cooks spoil the broth; 2) A bird in the hand is better than two birds in a bush; 3) When the cat's away, the mice will play; 4) Look before you leap; 5) You can't have your cake and eat it, too; 6) If you can't beat them, join them; 7) If the shoe fits, wear it; 8) You can't teach an old dog new tricks.* If time permits, discuss the meaning of unfamiliar proverbs.

19
LESSON

Taking Paraphrased Notes

Thebasiclawsofidealfrictionless
fluidsweregivenmathematicalformbyLeo
nhardEulerin1755.Eulerbasedhisworkinpa
rtonearlierworkbyDanielandJacquesBer
noulli.In1827,ClaudeNavierderivedtheequ
ationsofviscousflow,whichwerepublished
bySirGeorgeGabrielStokesin1845. . .

In Other Words . . .

Did you know that it's possible to hear more than 7,000 words in one hour of class time? That's a lot of words to hear, understand, and remember! Would you want—or be able—to write down every word while taking notes?

And think about all the words in all the books you are assigned to read. Did you know that an entire chapter of a book can be condensed into a page or two of notes? How can you do that? Easily! It's called *paraphrasing*.

Where Do You Stand?

Try this experiment. Find a couple of medium-sized paragraphs from one of your textbooks. On a separate sheet of paper, copy the paragraphs word-for-word, using a watch with a second hand to time yourself as you write. Then, time yourself as you take notes on the paragraphs again. This time, just write the most important ideas in your own words.

When you've completed the experiment, answer these questions:

1. What was the difference in your times?
2. How much of your fastest writing can you read?
3. How much of what you copied word-for-word is necessary information?
4. What conclusions can you draw from the experiment?

76 Level C • Achieve Mastery

Rate Yourself

Trying to take down every word isn't likely to work very well. The notes you took in your own words were probably quicker to write and easier to understand. Writing ideas in your own words is called *paraphrasing*.

Practice Oral Paraphrasing

With a partner, find out how good you are at listening and comprehending. Ask your partner to read a selection from a textbook or an encyclopedia. Sit and listen as your partner reads. Then use your own words to tell what has just been said. This might take a little practice! In time you'll get better at identifying and summing up the important ideas in what you have heard.

From oral paraphrasing, it's just a short step to paraphrasing as you take notes. Using a different selection, repeat the activity with your partner. This time, write paraphrased notes of what you hear on the lines below.

Familiar Ideas, Unfamiliar Words

Proverbs are familiar sayings. The proverbs below, however, have been rewritten to disguise them. Paraphrase these wordy versions by writing the familiar proverb on the lines below. Like all good paraphrasing, the familiar proverb is short and concise.

1. Superfluous chefs destroy the soup.
2. A member of the avian species in the fist is of more value than two members of the avian species in a shrub.
3. When the feline has departed, the rodents will cavort.
4. Survey the area before you jump.
5. You can't keep your angel food and devour it also.
6. If you can't overcome them, participate with them.
7. If the sandal is the correct size, put it on.
8. You can't educate an elderly canine to perform unfamiliar stunts.

Unit 6 • Participating in Class 77

Pages 78–79

- **Tips for Paraphrasing**
  Read the tips with your class. Students will discover that paraphrasing can be helpful in a variety of situations. They can paraphrase as they listen to keep up with the speaker's ideas. Paraphrasing as they take notes from reading can save valuable time as they research. It will also help as they use their research notes to prepare a report, since the ideas will already be in students' own words. You may want to use *Paraphrasing From Research* as a practice activity. Suggest that students cover page 79 with a sheet of paper and take notes about Wilma Rudolph. They can check their notes by comparing them with the sample paraphrased notes on page 79.
- **Where Are You Going?**
  Ask students to write a goal about ways they plan to use paraphrased notes as they listen and read.

Teacher Modeling

You may wish to use or adapt these examples of teacher modeling.

As I take paraphrased notes:

- I distinguish between important and unimportant information as I listen.
- I use my own words to record main ideas and important details.
- I use words and phrases instead of sentences.
- I write clearly and legibly so I'll be able to read my notes when I need them.
- I focus on the meaning of what the speaker is saying as I let my hands do the writing.

After taking notes:

- I review them as soon as possible.
- I make sure my notes are easy to read and well organized.
- I rewrite anything that may be unclear later.

Tips for Paraphrasing

Paraphrasing When Listening

- Don't try to make a word-for-word record of everything said in class. No matter what form your notes take, or whose words you are listening to, write down only the most important ideas or the facts you think you need to remember.
- Try to capture the speaker's meaning in as few words as possible. Leave out little words like *a*, *an*, and *the*. Use the & sign and other abbreviations.
- Don't paraphrase when the speaker's words include terms you need to remember. Use the terms and make sure you know how to spell them correctly.
- Concentrate on the main ideas of the presentation rather than on specific details.
- If there's something you don't quite understand, you may not be able to paraphrase. In that case, write down the speaker's exact words and surround them with quotation marks. Write a large question mark in the margin so you can come back and review the idea later.
- Try to catch vivid or striking words and phrases that your teacher uses. Write them down and use quotation marks. They'll help you reconstruct the lesson when you are studying from your notes.

Wilma Rudolph

Paraphrasing From Research

Paraphrasing is also a good technique to use when you're doing research. As you do your research, write the ideas and facts you plan to use in your own words on index cards. Also note the source of the information.

Sometimes you'll want to use a direct quote to make a point. Anytime you copy words without paraphrasing, remember to use quotation marks. Then when you use the quote in your speech or report, explain that the words are a direct quote and give the name of the author.

Read the excerpt about Olympic star Wilma Rudolph below. Then read the sample note cards on the next page. They show how you might take notes by paraphrasing and quoting different parts of the article.

Olympic All-Stars
Wilma Rudolph, Track and Field, 1960

When Wilma Rudolph was born, no one expected her to grow up to be an athlete. In fact, no one expected her to survive. The seventeenth child in a family of nineteen, Wilma was a very tiny baby. She lived her first few years as an invalid. Wilma had contracted polio when she was four. Doctors predicted that Rudolph would never walk again, but Rudolph's parents refused to accept the doctors' predictions, and the whole family worked together to help with little Wilma's therapy.

Rudolph learned to walk with a leg brace and then a special shoe. She refused to let her physical problems stop her. She qualified for the 1956 Olympics in track and field while she was still in high school. In 1960, she again went to the Summer Games. This time, she became the first American woman to win three gold medals in track. For this accomplishment, the Associated Press voted her U.S. Female Athlete of the Year. However, Rudolph's greatest victory was not at the Olympics; her greatest victory was her triumph over illness.

78 Level C • Achieve Mastery

Paraphrased Notes

This note card summarizes information from the article. The information is paraphrased.

Wilma Rudolph
- 17th of 19 children in family. Tiny baby, almost didn't survive.
- polio when she was 4 yrs. old, doctors said she'd never walk
- whole family worked to help her + she learned to walk again
- 1960 olympics – won 3 gold medals in track! (1st U.S. woman to do that)

Source: "Olympic All-Stars." Reading for Information. Columbus, OH: Zaner-Bloser, Inc., 1997, p. 93.

Direct Quotations

This note card records several direct quotations from the article. The words are placed in quotation marks.

Wilma Rudolph
"Rudolph learned to walk with a leg brace and then a special shoe. She refused to let her physical problems stop her."
"the Associated Press voted her U.S. Female Athlete of the Year."
"Rudolph's greatest victory was not at the olympics; her greatest victory was her triumph over illness."

Source: "Olympic All-Stars." Reading for Information. Columbus, OH: Zaner-Bloser, Inc., 1997, p. 93.

Where Are You Going?

Summarize what you learned in this lesson. __________

Now use your summary to write a *Take Charge!* goal that will help you become a better student.

Unit 6 • Participating in Class 79

20 LESSON Study Strategies for Reading

About Reading Study Strategies

Students need to understand that reading assignments carefully is just a beginning. Even more important is remembering what they have read. In this lesson, students will review the SQ3R and PRQT study methods. They'll also learn about PRQST, PROTO, and K-W-L charts. Each method is a unique approach to reading and retaining information. By exposing your students to a variety of reading study strategies, you'll be giving them the background they need to choose the study system that best fits their personal study style.

Pages 80–81

- **Letter Scramble**
After students read the lesson introduction, invite them to describe study methods they have used. Explain that learning a variety of study methods will help them choose the method that works best for them. Tell how you use similar strategies to recall important information (see *Teacher Modeling*).

- **Where Do You Stand?/Rate Yourself**
Even students who think they don't have any special study system may already be using some of the techniques they'll find in organized methods. After students complete the checklist, invite volunteers to tell why they use the techniques they checked. In a follow-up discussion, help students see that even though some of the steps take extra time initially, they save time in the long run.

- **Review SQ3R**
Review PRQT
Compare Study Methods
Students can work in small groups to review and compare SQ3R and PRQT. Suggest that they look for similarities and differences between the two methods and discuss which system takes longer and which one is likely to help them recall more information. Then ask students to make a personal choice between

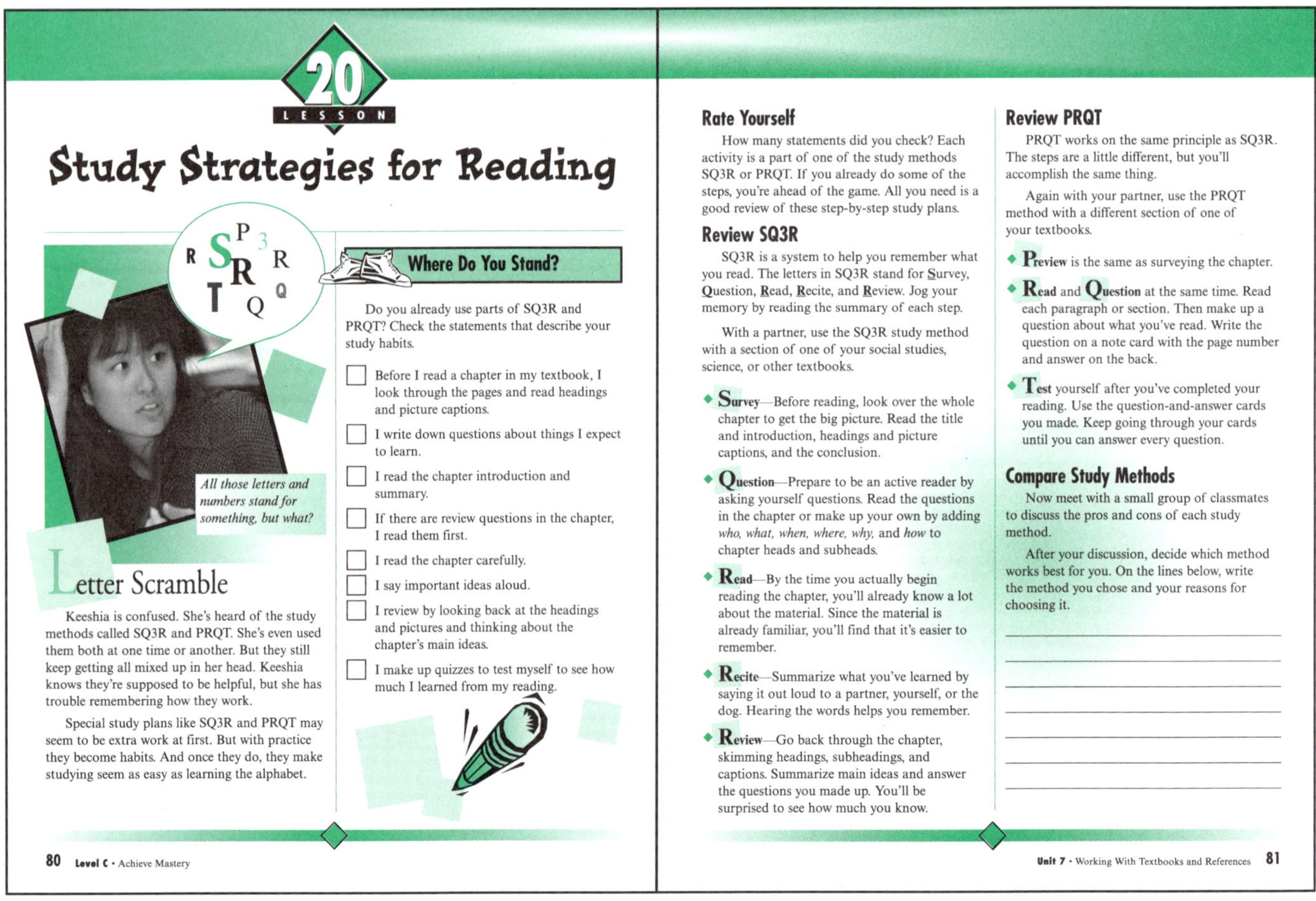

20 LESSON

Study Strategies for Reading

All those letters and numbers stand for something, but what?

Letter Scramble

Keeshia is confused. She's heard of the study methods called SQ3R and PRQT. She's even used them both at one time or another. But they still keep getting all mixed up in her head. Keeshia knows they're supposed to be helpful, but she has trouble remembering how they work.

Special study plans like SQ3R and PRQT may seem to be extra work at first. But with practice they become habits. And once they do, they make studying seem as easy as learning the alphabet.

Where Do You Stand?

Do you already use parts of SQ3R and PRQT? Check the statements that describe your study habits.

- ☐ Before I read a chapter in my textbook, I look through the pages and read headings and picture captions.
- ☐ I write down questions about things I expect to learn.
- ☐ I read the chapter introduction and summary.
- ☐ If there are review questions in the chapter, I read them first.
- ☐ I read the chapter carefully.
- ☐ I say important ideas aloud.
- ☐ I review by looking back at the headings and pictures and thinking about the chapter's main ideas.
- ☐ I make up quizzes to test myself to see how much I learned from my reading.

80 Level C • Achieve Mastery

Rate Yourself

How many statements did you check? Each activity is a part of one of the study methods SQ3R or PRQT. If you already do some of the steps, you're ahead of the game. All you need is a good review of these step-by-step study plans.

Review SQ3R

SQ3R is a system to help you remember what you read. The letters in SQ3R stand for Survey, Question, Read, Recite, and Review. Jog your memory by reading the summary of each step.

With a partner, use the SQ3R study method with a section of one of your social studies, science, or other textbooks.

- Survey—Before reading, look over the whole chapter to get the big picture. Read the title and introduction, headings and picture captions, and the conclusion.
- Question—Prepare to be an active reader by asking yourself questions. Read the questions in the chapter or make up your own by adding *who, what, when, where, why,* and *how* to chapter heads and subheads.
- Read—By the time you actually begin reading the chapter, you'll already know a lot about the material. Since the material is already familiar, you'll find that it's easier to remember.
- Recite—Summarize what you've learned by saying it out loud to a partner, yourself, or the dog. Hearing the words helps you remember.
- Review—Go back through the chapter, skimming headings, subheadings, and captions. Summarize main ideas and answer the questions you made up. You'll be surprised to see how much you know.

Review PRQT

PRQT works on the same principle as SQ3R. The steps are a little different, but you'll accomplish the same thing.

Again with your partner, use the PRQT method with a different section of one of your textbooks.

- Preview is the same as surveying the chapter.
- Read and Question at the same time. Read each paragraph or section. Then make up a question about what you've read. Write the question on a note card with the page number and answer on the back.
- Test yourself after you've completed your reading. Use the question-and-answer cards you made. Keep going through your cards until you can answer every question.

Compare Study Methods

Now meet with a small group of classmates to discuss the pros and cons of each study method.

After your discussion, decide which method works best for you. On the lines below, write the method you chose and your reasons for choosing it.

Unit 7 • Working With Textbooks and References 81

the two study methods. Discuss their choices.

Pages 82–83

- **More Study Methods**
  As students read about each study system, pause to allow them to compare the new method with the ones they already know. Call on volunteers to identify similarities and differences in the study methods and give situations in which each one might best be used. Make sure students understand that PROTO is particularly helpful when they read literature selections. A K-W-L chart is especially helpful when they are beginning a new chapter. The K-W-L chart can be adapted for research projects by adding an *H: How will you find out?*
- **Where Are You Going?**
  Ask students to write a goal for using a study method (or a combination of methods) to remember what they read.

Teacher Modeling

You may wish to use or adapt these examples of teacher modeling.

When I'm reading technical material:

- I skim over the material, paying special attention to pictures and diagrams, to get an idea of what the selection is all about.
- I read through the material carefully.
- I write down any questions I have. Then I look for the answers.

When I'm reading literature:

- I read the book blurb and information about the author.
- I look at pictures and chapter headings to get an idea of what might happen.
- I read for enjoyment.
- If I have trouble keeping track of the characters or following the plot, I take notes as I read.

More Study Methods

Find the Right Study System

PRQT and SQ3R are time-tested study systems. Over the years, many people have tried them out and modified them for their own purposes.

Here are some other study methods you may want to try. They're similar, but each one is a little different. Try each method on your own to find the one that's comfortable for you. Think carefully! The study method you choose now may be the one you use for the rest of your life.

PRQST

PRQST is almost the same as PRQT. It simply adds a step that you may find helpful.

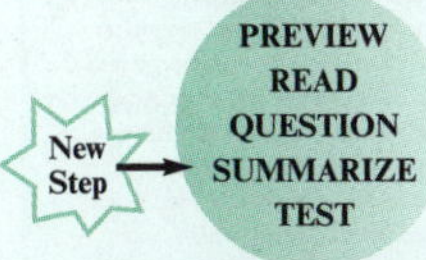

PREVIEW
READ
QUESTION
SUMMARIZE
TEST

PREVIEW, READ, and QUESTION just as you would for PRQT. But as you read, stop at the end of each section to take notes that SUMMARIZE what you've read. Review your notes before you move on to the final step in which you TEST yourself. You may be surprised at how much this one extra step adds to the PRQT system!

PROTO

SQ3R, PRQT, and PRQST are all good methods for reading chapters in textbooks or articles in reference materials. PROTO is a study technique that works with novels, short stories, and essays as well as with textbooks and articles. Read the description of this study method below. You might find it works well for you!

- **Preview** the material to get a grasp of the general idea. Pay careful attention to titles and headings.
- **Read** the material, watching for main ideas and key points. Read and reread as many times as you need to. When you feel that you understand the material, go on to the next step.
- **Organize** the information. Think about the way the information was presented and the best organizational strategy that you can use to recall the material. Choose from among strategies such as comparison and contrast, cause and effect, and sequence of events.
- **Take Notes** based on the organizational strategy you've selected. Graphic organizers are a great way to organize your notes. You might make an outline, a web, or a chart. Whatever you choose, make sure to list key points and details under the appropriate main ideas.
- **Overview** your notes when they're finished. Review and summarize to make sure you've got the big picture. Then fill in the details by reviewing the facts.

Give me a P. Give me an R. Give me an O. Give me a T. Give me another O!

82 **Level C** • Achieve Mastery

Make a K-W-L Chart

When using the K-W-L technique, start by making a chart like the one below. Before reading, brainstorm what you already KNOW about the subject. Write your ideas in the first column. Then think as specifically as you can about what you WANT to find out from your reading. Write your questions in the second column. When you've finished reading, fill in the LEARN column with the new things you've learned.

K-W-L is a process for studying. If you find out that any of the ideas in the KNOW column were incorrect, make a note of that, too. You may find that the new things you learn raise even more questions. If so, revise the second column of your chart.

What I KNOW	What I WANT to Know	What I LEARNED

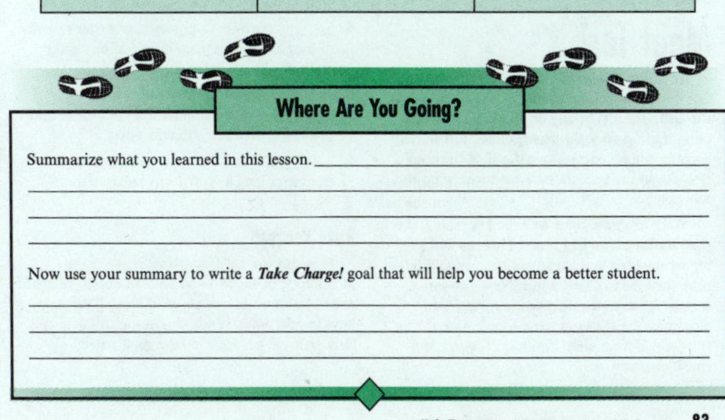

Where Are You Going?

Summarize what you learned in this lesson. ______________________________

Now use your summary to write a ***Take Charge!*** goal that will help you become a better student.

____

Unit 7 • Working With Textbooks and References 83

Taking Notes From Reading

About Reading and Note-Taking

Your students probably realize that there's more to taking good notes than copying words from a book. But they may not know that using someone else's copyrighted words is a crime like shoplifting. Most students don't set out to plagiarize, but they can find themselves guilty of plagiarism through inattention or carelessness. In this lesson, students will learn note-taking techniques that will help them take useful notes and, at the same time, guard against inadvertent plagiarism.

Pages 84–85

- **Meet Teri**
  Students may feel that what happened to Teri is unfair. Help them understand that plagiarism is unfair to an author, even when it is done out of carelessness or ignorance. Explain that the same strategies that help them take useful notes will also keep them from plagiarizing accidentally. Then share your own strategies for taking notes from reading (see *Teacher Modeling*).
- **Where Do You Stand?/Rate Yourself**
  Suggest that students assess their understanding of plagiarism by taking the quiz.
- **Practice Taking Notes**
  To get a concrete picture of the difference between paraphrasing and plagiarizing, let students work on their own to take notes on the article about the food chain on the savanna. Then they can work with partners to compare their notes to the original text and underline or highlight phrases or sentences that come right out of the article. Put examples of good note-taking on the board. If any students are willing to share examples of inadvertent plagiarism, read the examples and then work together to correct them.

Taking Notes From Reading

Meet Teri

Teri has a problem. One night she stayed up late to do research for a report. As she grew tired, the notes she was taking changed. Instead of paraphrasing what she was reading, Teri started copying whole sentences right out of the book. She was so tired she didn't even notice what she was doing.

When the time came to write her report, she used the notes she had taken. Parts of Teri's report sounded familiar to her teacher, and he took the time to check it out. Now Teri's in trouble for using another writer's words, or *plagiarizing*. Following some simple note-taking rules would have saved Teri lots of worry and embarrassment.

Where Do You Stand?

Could you find yourself in Teri's shoes? Take this quiz to find out how well you understand the rules for note-taking. Write *True* or *False* before each statement.

1. ______ Plagiarizing is using another writer's words as your own.
2. ______ Plagiarizing refers only to copying from another classmate's paper.
3. ______ It's okay to use information you find in a book as long as you put it in your own words and identify the original source.
4. ______ It's okay to use another writer's words as long as you put them in quotation marks and tell who wrote them.
5. ______ One way to avoid accidental plagiarizing is to paraphrase, or put ideas into your own words, as you take notes.
6. ______ Plagiarizing won't cause you any trouble as long as you didn't mean to do it.

Rate Yourself

How did you do? If you answered *True* to questions 1, 3, 4, and 5 and *False* to questions 2 and 6, you probably have a good idea of the right ways to take notes. If not, this lesson will help you learn to avoid trouble and take good notes.

84 **Level C** • Achieve Mastery

Practice Taking Notes

Read the article at the bottom of the page. On the lines in the next column, write a summary of what you read.

When you are finished, work with a partner to compare the summaries you wrote with the original article. Did either of you plagiarize, or copy whole parts of the text word-for-word? It's okay to use some words and phrases from the article. Just make sure you used your own words to explain the main ideas.

____
____
____
____
____
____
____
____
____

The Savanna Food Chain

Animals of the Savanna

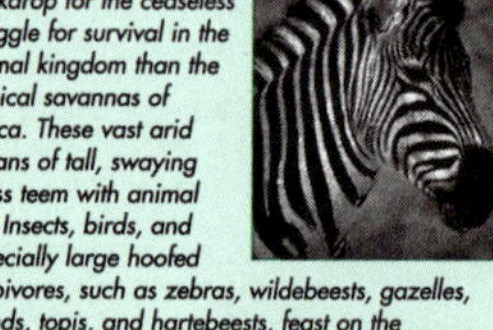

No biome on Earth provides a more dramatic backdrop for the ceaseless struggle for survival in the animal kingdom than the tropical savannas of Africa. These vast arid oceans of tall, swaying grass teem with animal life. Insects, birds, and especially large hoofed herbivores, such as zebras, wildebeests, gazelles, elands, topis, and hartebeests, feast on the abundant vegetation, while carnivores —lions, cheetahs, leopards, and African wild dogs—crouch low in the grasses, waiting for the opportunity to pounce. Scavengers pace restlessly nearby or hover in the blue sky above, anxiously waiting to devour what remains when the carnivores have eaten their fill. The plants, herbivores, carnivores, and scavengers of the savanna provide an ideal example of an ecosystem in action.

The Food Chain

The term "food chain" is used to describe the way energy from the sun is transferred from one life form to another, changing form along the way. This is how the food chain of the savanna works: First, energy from the sun is collected by grasses and other plants, which use the sun's energy and the process of photosynthesis to manufacture sugars and starches. Next, the plants are eaten by herbivores, whose bodies become repositories for the nutritional components obtained from the plants. Herbivores, in turn, are devoured by carnivores, which, under normal conditions, take only the most nutritious parts of their prey. Whatever remains after the carnivores are finished is taken by scavengers. Nothing is wasted in the savanna food chain, because what is left by scavengers serves to fertilize the soil, which, in turn, nourishes new plant life.

Unit 7 • Working With Textbooks and References 85

Pages 86–87

- **Tips for Careful Note-Taking**
  Ask a volunteer to read each tip aloud. Encourage students to find the copyright notices in classroom books. Read one of the notices aloud and help students interpret it and put it into their own words. Remind students that by taking notes in short phrases they have put into their own words, they'll not only be avoiding plagiarism, but will also be taking good, useful notes. You may wish to work together as a class to practice the *Scan and Chunk* technique on a textbook passage.
- **Note-Taking DOs and DON'Ts**
  Ask students to read the two lists. Invite volunteers to add their own ideas and to summarize the rules for avoiding plagiarism.
- **Where Are You Going?**
  Ask students to write a goal that includes changes they plan to make in the way they take notes from reading.

Teacher Modeling

You may wish to use or adapt these examples of teacher modeling.

When I take notes as I read:

- I paraphrase by putting the author's ideas into my own words.
- I summarize the main ideas of a long passage by writing no more than a sentence or two.
- When I'm doing research, I record separate facts and ideas on individual index cards.

To make sure I don't accidentally plagiarize:

- I make sure I really understand an idea before I write it.
- I use synonyms for words the author used, and I use a thesaurus for help if I need it.
- I avoid writing complete sentences.
- I use quotation marks and give credit if I need to use an author's words to make a point.

Tips for Careful Note-Taking

Copyrights and Wrongs

Have you ever noticed the copyright on a book? Usually it is located in the front of the book on the back side of the title page. Copyrights are a form of protection for writers and artists. It protects the works they create.

When a piece of writing is copyrighted, it means it is the property of the author, just like a bicycle or a television is the property of the person who owns it. No one else can publish that piece of writing without obtaining the permission of the author. If you use a writer's work word-for-word in your paper without quotation marks and without giving the author credit, you are stealing something that belongs to someone else. Almost everything you read or take notes from is copyrighted, so be careful!

A Dictionary Can Help

You're most likely to copy right out of the book when you don't understand an idea well enough to put it into your own words. Before you write any notes, make sure you understand the ideas. Look up unfamiliar words in the dictionary. If you're running short of time or don't have a dictionary handy, copy the words from the book and put them in quotation marks. Later, when you have more time and access to a dictionary, rewrite the words in quotation marks into your own words.

Scan and Chunk

Scan your assignment. Then read it in small chunks. Scanning will help you find out what you're supposed to know. Chunking will help you digest the information a little bit at a time. Taking notes about a chunk of information, instead of sentence by sentence, will help you keep from inadvertently copying ideas word-for-word.

3 x 5 = Power

Use the power of the 3 x 5 index card. These cards are especially useful when you are writing a report or doing a research paper. Create a source card for every source of information you use, whether it's a book, a newspaper or magazine article, an interview, an audiotape, or any other research material.

Then take your notes, writing only one piece of information on each card. Record the source of the information on the card. Then sort your cards to construct an outline for your paper. If you're using more than one source, make sure ideas from different sources are mixed together.

Turn back to page 79. The illustration shows note cards—one with paraphrased information and one that quotes directly from the source. You can use these cards as a model when you make your own.

86 Level C • Achieve Mastery

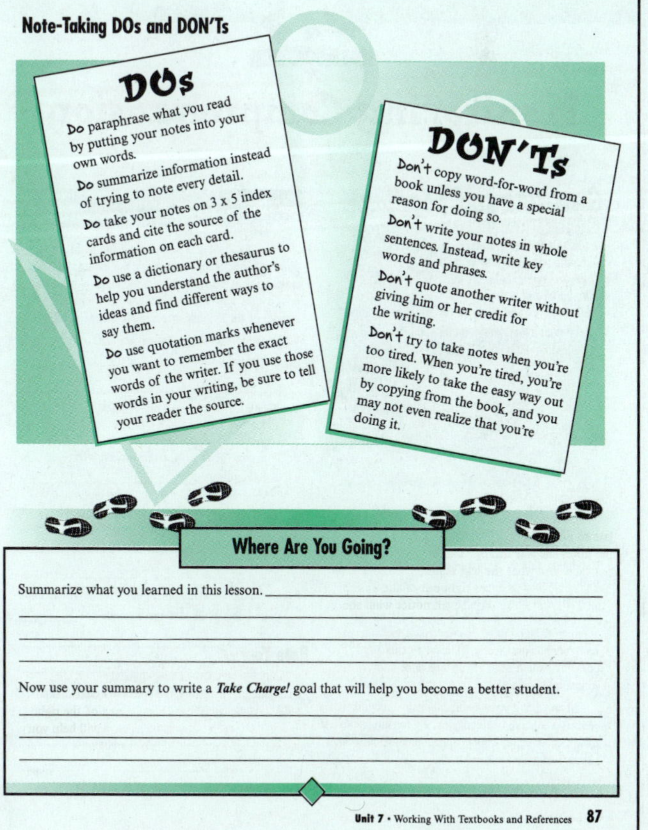
Note-Taking DOs and DON'Ts

DOs

Do paraphrase what you read by putting your notes into your own words.

Do summarize information instead of trying to note every detail.

Do take your notes on 3 x 5 index cards and cite the source of the information on each card.

Do use a dictionary or thesaurus to help you understand the author's ideas and find different ways to say them.

Do use quotation marks whenever you want to remember the exact words of the writer. If you use those words in your writing, be sure to tell your reader the source.

DON'Ts

Don't copy word-for-word from a book unless you have a special reason for doing so.

Don't write your notes in whole sentences. Instead, write key words and phrases.

Don't quote another writer without giving him or her credit for the writing.

Don't try to take notes when you're too tired. When you're tired, you're more likely to take the easy way out by copying from the book, and you may not even realize that you're doing it.

Where Are You Going?

Summarize what you learned in this lesson. ______

Now use your summary to write a *Take Charge!* goal that will help you become a better student. ______

Unit 7 • Working With Textbooks and References 87

Monitoring Comprehension

About Monitoring

All of us sometimes find our minds wandering as we read. The key to good comprehension is recognizing that we've been daydreaming and rereading to correct the situation. When students are unaware that their attention has lapsed, they miss important bits of information without even knowing it. In this lesson, students will learn to monitor their focus and comprehension so they can backtrack to pick up information they've missed.

Pages 88–89

◆ **Give Yourself Feedback**
Without prior discussion, tell students to read the lesson introduction to themselves. When they finish, they can move right on to *Where Do You Stand?*

◆ **Where Do You Stand?/Rate Yourself**
After students complete *Where Do You Stand?*, invite volunteers to share their answers to the questions and respond to the questions asked in *Rate Yourself*. Allow time for students to tell how they know when they've been letting their eyes travel across the page instead of thinking about what they read. Tell some of your strategies for monitoring your reading comprehension and maintaining focus (see *Teacher Modeling*).

◆ **Be Aware**
Keep Your Focus
Encourage students to work with partners to become human biofeedback machines that monitor their awareness as they read. Then let pairs practice tuning out distractions. Invite students to note the kinds of distractions that bothered them the most and to discuss how being aware of their own level of concentration can cut down on homework time and improve school performance.

22 LESSON

Monitoring Comprehension

Give Yourself Feedback

A biofeedback machine uses sensors similar to these to monitor subtle changes in the body and provide feedback for the patient.

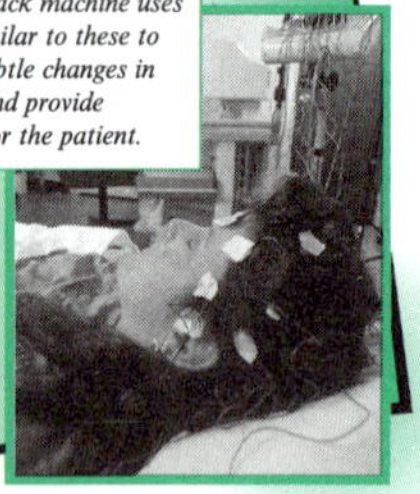

Have you ever heard of *biofeedback*? Biofeedback is a medical technique that uses special equipment to monitor bodily functions like heart rate or blood pressure. The theory behind biofeedback is that by constantly monitoring, or being aware of, what is going on inside his or her own body, a patient can learn to take control. Biofeedback techniques have been found to be effective in treating conditions like high blood pressure and migraine headaches.

Monitoring your comprehension as you read is a lot like biofeedback. By making yourself aware of your reading comprehension, you take control of your own learning.

Where Do You Stand?

You don't need a fancy machine to monitor your reading comprehension. You just need to train your mind to focus on the right things. See how aware you were as you read the lesson introduction by answering these questions.

1. Were you feeling calm or nervous as you read the introduction? ____________
2. Was your body tense or relaxed? ____________
3. Did you focus your attention on what you were reading? ____________
4. Describe all the sounds you could hear as you read. ____________
5. Describe the stray thoughts that went through your head while you were reading. ____________
6. Without rereading the first paragraph, define *biofeedback*. ____________

88 Level C • Achieve Mastery

Rate Yourself

How did you do? Were you aware of the feelings you had while you read? Did noises and stray thoughts distract you?

Unfortunately, unlike biofeedback, there is no special equipment to monitor your focus and comprehension. But there are strategies that you can learn and use, strategies that will help you improve your comprehension skills. Read on to find out more.

Be Aware

Find a partner to be your biofeedback machine. Tell your partner to stop you at random intervals while you read a textbook selection. Each time your partner stops you, write a brief summary of what you've just read on the lines below. If your mind was wandering while you read, write down what you were thinking about instead. If you were aware that you weren't concentrating on your reading, make a star beside your description.

1. ____________
2. ____________
3. ____________
4. ____________

Keep Your Focus

Here's your chance to break some rules and see what happens. Select a textbook chapter you haven't read yet. Then ask a partner to try to distract you as you read. Your partner may hum, talk, tap pencils, or do anything that is not so loud that it distracts the rest of the class. Your partner may not touch you. When you finish reading, answer the questions.

1. What was the main idea of what you read? ____________
2. Name three details you recall. ____________
3. Write three things you read in order. ____________
4. What was the most distracting thing your partner did? ____________
5. What techniques helped you maintain your concentration? ____________

Unit 7 • Working With Textbooks and References 89

Pages 90–91

◆ **Learn to Shift Gears**
When You Just Can't Concentrate…
Read and discuss these tips for monitoring comprehension with the students. Encourage them to use the self-questioning technique when reading textbooks. Ask students to suggest additional ways to refocus when they're having trouble concentrating.

◆ **Monitor Information Flow**
Write It Down
Explain that information can enter the brain through different paths. The more pathways students use, the more likely they are to recall what they read later. Encourage students to experiment with ways to use auditory and kinesthetic methods to help them remember what they read.

◆ **Where Are You Going?**
Ask students to write a goal for monitoring their comprehension as they read.

Teacher Modeling

You may wish to use or adapt these examples of teacher modeling.

To keep my attention from wandering as I read:

- I read actively.
- I restate important ideas in my own words.
- I try to predict what will happen next.

To monitor information flow:

- I pause often to summarize what I'm reading.
- I say the main points aloud to myself.
- I try to explain the ideas to someone else.
- I write down the important ideas.

After I finish reading:

- I review to check for knowledge gaps.
- I quiz myself on what I have read.
- I relate the new information to things I already know.

Tips for Monitoring Comprehension as You Read

Learn to Shift Gears

Attentive drivers constantly shift their eyes from the road ahead to the rearview mirror. Even though their main goal is to stay on the road and out of the way of other cars, they need to be aware of what's going on around them at all times.

Monitoring comprehension works the same way. The best way to make sure you're understanding what you read is to take frequent glances at your mental rearview mirror. This means you check your comprehension at the end of every chapter, every section, or even every paragraph if the material is difficult. Each time you glance into that mental mirror, ask yourself these questions:

- Can I put the ideas into my own words?
- Do I need to look up any vocabulary words?
- Do I understand how the new information fits in with information I've learned before?
- Should I read some sections over again?
- Can I predict what will happen next?

If there are some things you didn't fully understand, go back and reread. If there are words you don't know, look them up. Make a prediction about what's coming next, then read on to see if your prediction was correct.

When You Just Can't Concentrate . . .

Monitoring your comprehension is the key to knowing when you're wasting time by just letting your eyes flow over the page without engaging your mind. Often just realizing that your mind is wandering can be enough to bring your attention back to the page. When it's not, try these tips.

- **Take a short break.** Maybe your mind is just too tired or overloaded with facts to keep going. If you're at home, get up and walk to another room or get a healthy snack. If you're at school, stretch at your seat, look around the room, and then get back to work.
- **Switch subjects.** If you don't have time for a break, give yourself a change of pace instead. Stop reading and do some math problems or write that poem for English class. When your mind feels more relaxed, you can get back to your reading.
- **Change your environment.** If you're at home, get up and move to another room. Move from a soft chair to a hard one. Turn off the radio or television. If you're at school, changing your environment will be harder. But you can do it by refocusing your attention, blocking out the distractions, and imagining yourself in another place.
- **Check for mental blocks.** Is a bad feeling holding you back? Maybe you got a bad grade on your last quiz, so you're nervous about the next one. Maybe you don't like the subject, the teacher, or even the person who sits beside you in class, so you don't like to go there. Figure out what's causing your mental block. Once you do that, it's likely to go away.

90 **Level C** • Achieve Mastery

Monitor Information Flow

Monitor the way information flows through your mind as you work. Monitoring information flow means taking what you've read and moving it through different parts of your brain to make it a permanent part of your personal data bank. Methods for monitoring information flow include:

- Summarizing the information in your mind
- Saying it out loud to yourself in your own words
- Writing it down
- Explaining it to another person

Write It Down

Writing information down is important for two reasons. The obvious reason is that, by taking notes or making an outline, you will have something permanent to refer to in case you forget what you've read. The more important reason, though, is that writing information down is the most effective way of processing new information. Just the act of writing it out will help transfer the new information from your short-term to your long-term memory. And that's the secret to turning information from a book into personal knowledge.

Explaining what you have read to another person is a great way to monitor the information you are learning.

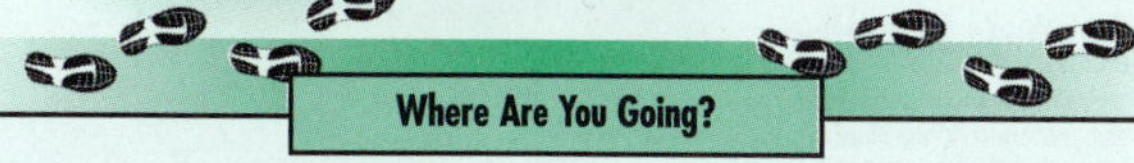

Where Are You Going?

Summarize what you learned in this lesson. ______________________

Now use your summary to write a *Take Charge!* goal that will help you become a better student.

Unit 7 • Working With Textbooks and References 91

Lesson 23 — Revising Notes

About Revising

Taking notes is a good way for students to remember what they read, but writing down notes is only the first step. Raw notes are like any first draft. Before students can get the most from their notes, they need to clarify, refine, and fill in gaps. Then they need to organize the information into a usable form. The extra steps result in an end product students can really use. The purpose of this lesson is to teach students that the revision process will help them remember what they read.

Pages 92–93

◆ **Get Involved in Your Reading**
After students read the introduction, discuss the two proverbs. They come from very different cultures. What do their similarities tell us about human nature? Help students relate the proverbs to note-taking. Students who just read or listen once are likely to forget. If they take notes they'll have something they can look at to remember. But working with the notes is the step that leads to real understanding.

◆ **Where Do You Stand?/Rate Yourself**
Ask students to complete the chart to help them think about what they do when they revise their notes. Invite volunteers to tell about their own note-taking techniques and how they adapt different strategies to different kinds of classroom and textbook notes. Share some ways you take and revise notes (see *Teacher Modeling*).

◆ **Sort It Out**
After students have revised Kevin's raw notes, suggest they get together in small groups to compare their revision techniques. Did students identify the same main ideas? Why did some choose to make an outline and others choose to make a web? If time permits, ask several students to copy their revised notes onto the board. Discuss why the more organized, revised notes would make a more useful study aid for Kevin.

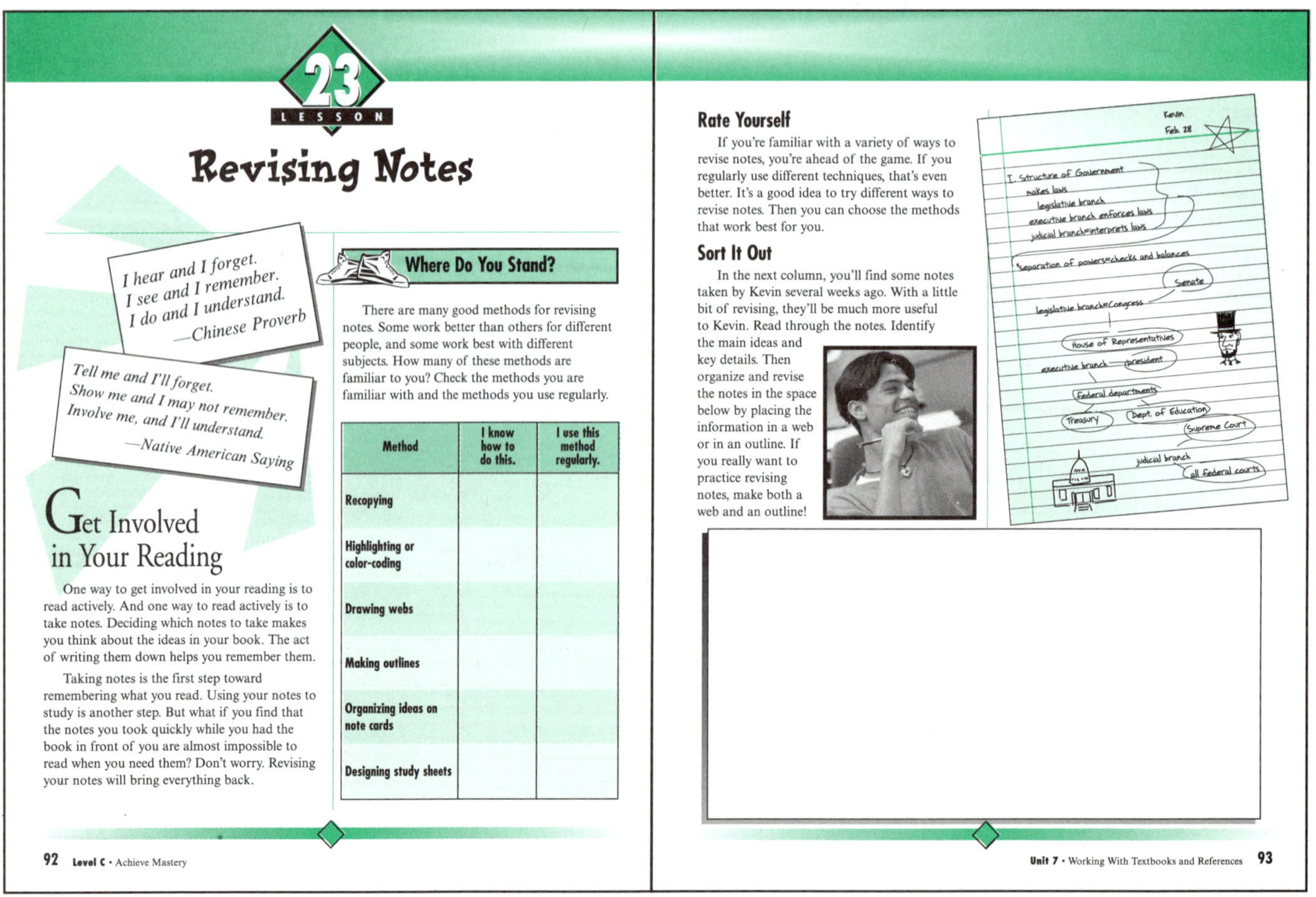

23 LESSON

Revising Notes

I hear and I forget.
I see and I remember.
I do and I understand.
—Chinese Proverb

Tell me and I'll forget.
Show me and I may not remember.
Involve me, and I'll understand.
—Native American Saying

Get Involved in Your Reading

One way to get involved in your reading is to read actively. And one way to read actively is to take notes. Deciding which notes to take makes you think about the ideas in your book. The act of writing them down helps you remember them.

Taking notes is the first step toward remembering what you read. Using your notes to study is another step. But what if you find that the notes you took quickly while you had the book in front of you are almost impossible to read when you need them? Don't worry. Revising your notes will bring everything back.

Where Do You Stand?

There are many good methods for revising notes. Some work better than others for different people, and some work best with different subjects. How many of these methods are familiar to you? Check the methods you are familiar with and the methods you use regularly.

Method	I know how to do this.	I use this method regularly.
Recopying		
Highlighting or color-coding		
Drawing webs		
Making outlines		
Organizing ideas on note cards		
Designing study sheets		

92 Level C • Achieve Mastery

Rate Yourself

If you're familiar with a variety of ways to revise notes, you're ahead of the game. If you regularly use different techniques, that's even better. It's a good idea to try different ways to revise notes. Then you can choose the methods that work best for you.

Sort It Out

In the next column, you'll find some notes taken by Kevin several weeks ago. With a little bit of revising, they'll be much more useful to Kevin. Read through the notes. Identify the main ideas and key details. Then organize and revise the notes in the space below by placing the information in a web or in an outline. If you really want to practice revising notes, make both a web and an outline!

Unit 7 • Working With Textbooks and References 93

Pages 94–95

- **Methods for Revising Notes**
There are many ways to rewrite notes. Recopying, while helpful, is least effective because it requires little thought. Making an outline or an organizer is a matter of personal preference. Remind students that they may want to vary their method according to the structure of the material and their purpose for revising. Kinesthetic learners may find that manipulating individual cards works best for them. Organizing note cards can also be the first step in making an outline or web.

- **Turn Your Notes Into Study Sheets**
Making study sheets will help students get the big picture and save time when they sit down to study.

- **Where Are You Going?**
Ask students to write a goal for improving their comprehension by revising their notes.

Teacher Modeling

You may wish to use or adapt these examples of teacher modeling.

When I take notes as I read:

- I write down main ideas and important details without worrying about how my notes look or are organized.
- I write clearly and legibly so I won't need to go back to the book to find out what I wrote.

To revise my notes:

- I reread my notes to make sure my ideas are clear.
- I look back in the book if I'm not sure what my notes meant or if I need to fill in gaps.
- I plan the best way to reorganize my notes.
- I rewrite them neatly.
- I organize notes from different sources on the same topic in one place.

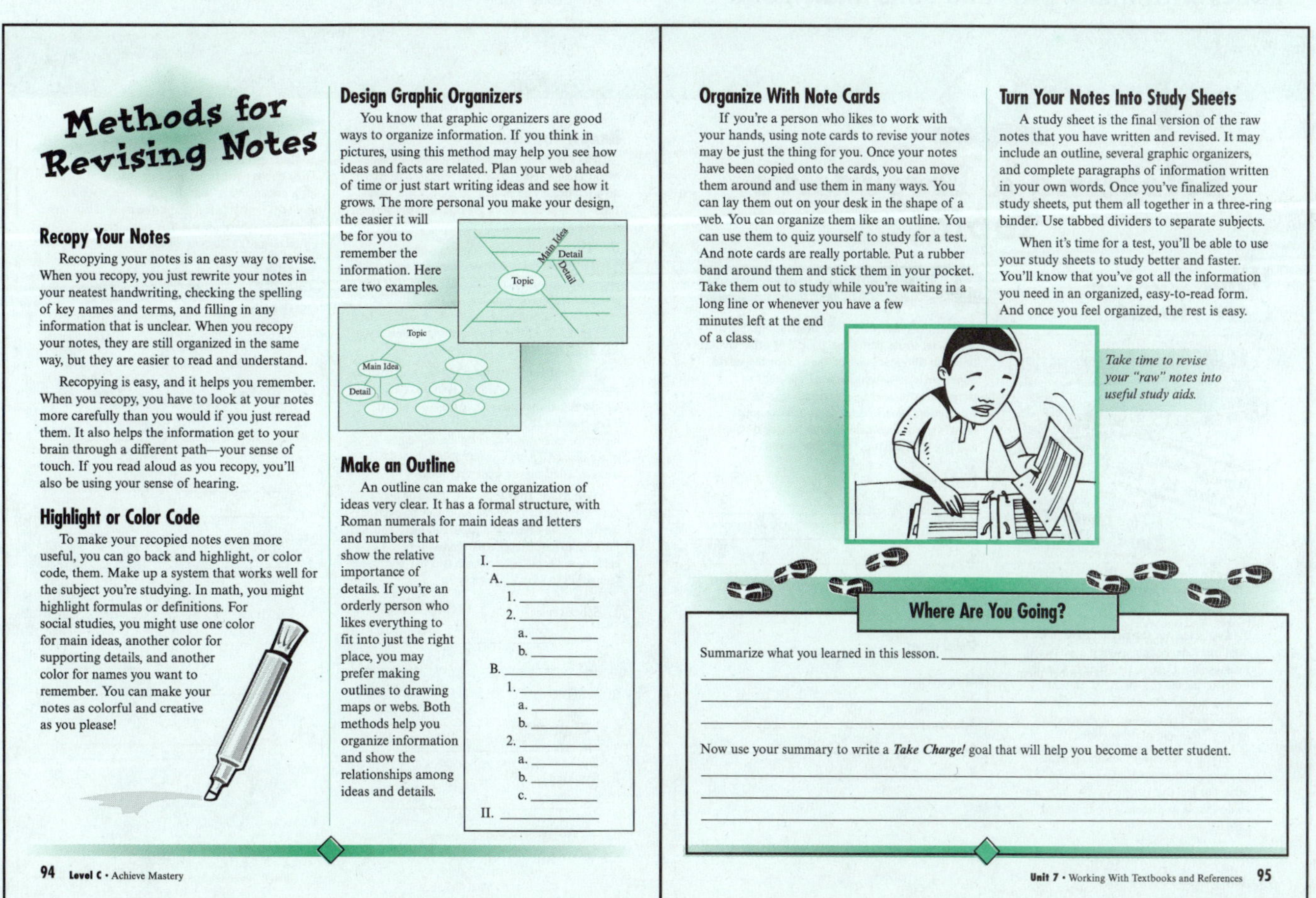

Methods for Revising Notes

Recopy Your Notes

Recopying your notes is an easy way to revise. When you recopy, you just rewrite your notes in your neatest handwriting, checking the spelling of key names and terms, and filling in any information that is unclear. When you recopy your notes, they are still organized in the same way, but they are easier to read and understand.

Recopying is easy, and it helps you remember. When you recopy, you have to look at your notes more carefully than you would if you just reread them. It also helps the information get to your brain through a different path—your sense of touch. If you read aloud as you recopy, you'll also be using your sense of hearing.

Highlight or Color Code

To make your recopied notes even more useful, you can go back and highlight, or color code, them. Make up a system that works well for the subject you're studying. In math, you might highlight formulas or definitions. For social studies, you might use one color for main ideas, another color for supporting details, and another color for names you want to remember. You can make your notes as colorful and creative as you please!

Design Graphic Organizers

You know that graphic organizers are good ways to organize information. If you think in pictures, using this method may help you see how ideas and facts are related. Plan your web ahead of time or just start writing ideas and see how it grows. The more personal you make your design, the easier it will be for you to remember the information. Here are two examples.

Make an Outline

An outline can make the organization of ideas very clear. It has a formal structure, with Roman numerals for main ideas and letters and numbers that show the relative importance of details. If you're an orderly person who likes everything to fit into just the right place, you may prefer making outlines to drawing maps or webs. Both methods help you organize information and show the relationships among ideas and details.

I. ______
  A. ______
    1. ______
    2. ______
      a. ______
      b. ______
  B. ______
    1. ______
      a. ______
      b. ______
    2. ______
      a. ______
      b. ______
      c. ______
II. ______

94 Level C • Achieve Mastery

Organize With Note Cards

If you're a person who likes to work with your hands, using note cards to revise your notes may be just the thing for you. Once your notes have been copied onto the cards, you can move them around and use them in many ways. You can lay them out on your desk in the shape of a web. You can organize them like an outline. You can use them to quiz yourself to study for a test. And note cards are really portable. Put a rubber band around them and stick them in your pocket. Take them out to study while you're waiting in a long line or whenever you have a few minutes left at the end of a class.

Turn Your Notes Into Study Sheets

A study sheet is the final version of the raw notes that you have written and revised. It may include an outline, several graphic organizers, and complete paragraphs of information written in your own words. Once you've finalized your study sheets, put them all together in a three-ring binder. Use tabbed dividers to separate subjects.

When it's time for a test, you'll be able to use your study sheets to study better and faster. You'll know that you've got all the information you need in an organized, easy-to-read form. And once you feel organized, the rest is easy.

Take time to revise your "raw" notes into useful study aids.

Where Are You Going?

Summarize what you learned in this lesson. ______

Now use your summary to write a *Take Charge!* goal that will help you become a better student. ______

Unit 7 • Working With Textbooks and References 95

Selecting a Persuasive Topic

About Persuasive Topics

Deciding on a good topic for a persuasive paper or project can be especially challenging for middle school students. They may find it fairly easy to identify broad issues and controversies that interest them. However, they will likely find it difficult to sort out all the arguments surrounding the issues and choose a specific focus for their work. The goal of this lesson is to introduce persuasive topics and to provide students with techniques for planning a focused, convincing argument.

Pages 96–97

- **What Do You Care About?**
  After students read the introduction, hold a brief discussion of current events. Summarize by having students decide which issues generated the most interest and which issues students disagreed about most. Suggest that issues with many pros and cons make good topics for persuasive reports and projects.

- **Where Do You Stand?**
  As students make their lists, encourage them to include issues discussed in class as well as other issues that are important to them. Ask students to write numbers beside their list items to rank them in order of interest and importance.

- **Narrow Your Topic**
  Organize Your Arguments
  Before students complete *Narrow Your Topic,* explain that students often make the mistake of choosing topics that are too broad to cover adequately. Share your own steps for selecting and narrowing a topic (see *Teacher Modeling*). Have students choose one narrowed topic they wrote to use for *Organize Your Arguments*. Ask students to think about how they might acknowledge or refute "cons" in a persuasive report. If time permits, invite students who wrote about similar topics to use their arguments in a debate.

24
LESSON

Selecting a Persuasive Topic

What Do You Care About?

Air Pollution Reaches Record High

Researchers Claim Link Between Nuclear Plant and Leukemia

Female Executives Still Earn 20% Less

The Last Tigers on the Planet?

What issues do you feel strongly about?

Issues are hot topics that have more than one side. People usually have strong feelings about issues, and they're usually ready to debate the issues, or present arguments for either side. Issues can be global, like preservation of rain forests, or local, like school dress codes.

If you feel strongly about an issue, chances are that you'd like to convince others to feel the same way. The only way to do that is to present a clear, logical case for your side.

Where Do You Stand?

There are many issues to think about. Some are global issues that affect people or other living things in different parts of the U.S. or the world. Some are local issues that are important to people in your town, your neighborhood, or even your school. What issues do you care about most? On the lines below, write five local issues and five global issues that concern you.

Local Issues

1. __________
2. __________
3. __________
4. __________
5. __________

Global Issues

1. __________
2. __________
3. __________
4. __________
5. __________

96 **Level C** • Achieve Mastery

Narrow Your Topic

The Problem: Mrs. Munoz gave this assignment: Give a report that will persuade people to do something worthwhile. Ramon, Gita, and Ellie thought this was a great idea. They formed a group and chose the topic *saving endangered species.*

But things started to go wrong almost right away. One group member complained that they couldn't really solve such a big problem. The others were afraid they could never even make a dent in reading all the background material that was available. What could they do?

The Solution: The group sat down to discuss the problem. As they talked, Ramon, Gita, and Ellie realized that their topic was too broad. They decided to make it narrower and closer to home. After they decided on the topic *how to make the local pond a good habitat for wild animals,* their report went smoothly.

Your Turn: Your topic can make or break your project. Too broad a topic can be overwhelming. Too narrow a topic can leave you with nothing to say. Practice narrowing topics. For each broad topic below, write two narrow topics you could use for a report.

1. School rules
   a. __________
   b. __________
2. Pollution
   a. __________
   b. __________
3. Smoking
   a. __________
   b. __________

Organize Your Arguments

Discuss the topics you wrote with a partner. Then choose one topic and organize your ideas for a persuasive speech. Begin with a statement that tells how you feel about the issue. Then write three *pros,* or arguments that support your opinion, and three *cons,* or arguments against your opinion.

Statement __________

Pros	Cons
a.	a.
b.	b.
c.	c.

Unit 8 • Preparing Speeches, Reports, and Projects 97

Pages 98–99

- **Tips for Choosing Your Best Topic**
  Ask a volunteer to read each section aloud. Students need to understand that they will probably try out several different topics before committing to one. On these two pages, students will find a reliable process they can use to evaluate potential topics. Have students complete the *Topic Report Card* for one or two topics they worked with on page 97.
- **Your Project Notebook—Your Most Important Resource**
  If students will use this and the following lessons to prepare an actual speech, report, or project, make sure to discuss the importance of a project notebook. Have students create their notebooks before the next lesson.
- **Where Are You Going?**
  Ask students to write a goal that will help them choose persuasive topics in the future.

Teacher Modeling

You may wish to use or adapt these examples of teacher modeling.

To brainstorm potential topics:

- I watch the news, read magazines, and talk to others to identify "hot topics."
- I think about issues I care about most and topics I'd like to explore.
- I make a list or a web to show my ideas.

To narrow a topic:

- I choose a focus that will be interesting to me and my audience.
- I make my topic fit the requirements of the assignment.
- I find out what research material is available.
- I choose a topic I can cover adequately in the time and space allowed.

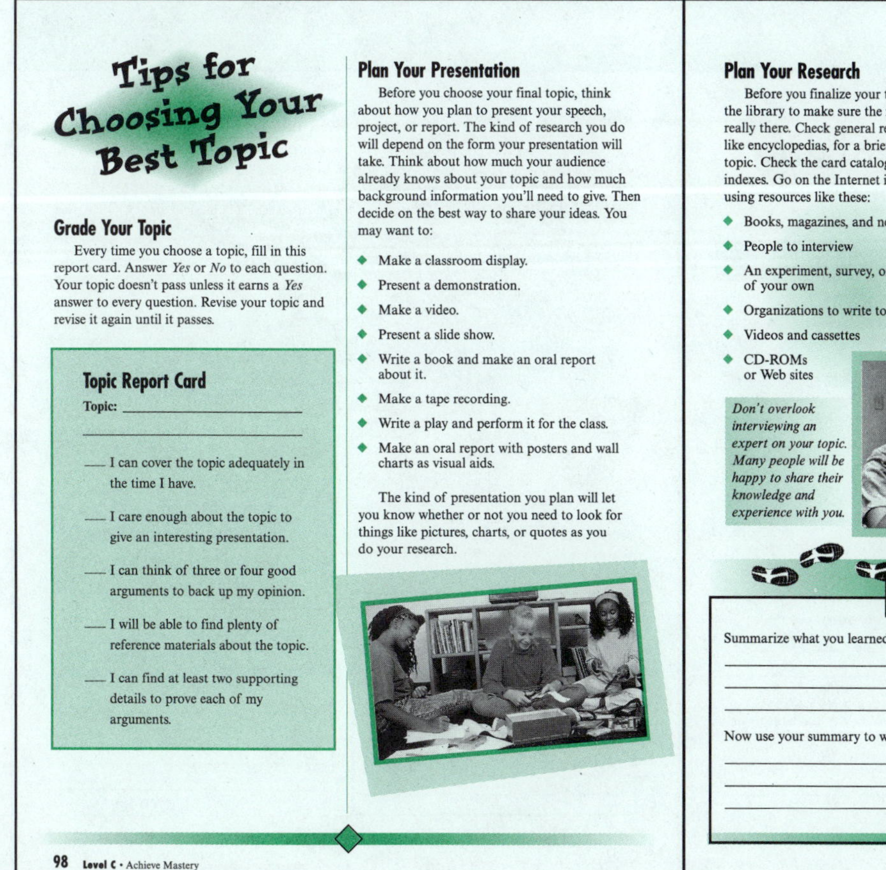

Tips for Choosing Your Best Topic

Grade Your Topic

Every time you choose a topic, fill in this report card. Answer *Yes* or *No* to each question. Your topic doesn't pass unless it earns a *Yes* answer to every question. Revise your topic and revise it again until it passes.

Topic Report Card

Topic: ____________________

____ I can cover the topic adequately in the time I have.

____ I care enough about the topic to give an interesting presentation.

____ I can think of three or four good arguments to back up my opinion.

____ I will be able to find plenty of reference materials about the topic.

____ I can find at least two supporting details to prove each of my arguments.

Plan Your Presentation

Before you choose your final topic, think about how you plan to present your speech, project, or report. The kind of research you do will depend on the form your presentation will take. Think about how much your audience already knows about your topic and how much background information you'll need to give. Then decide on the best way to share your ideas. You may want to:

- Make a classroom display.
- Present a demonstration.
- Make a video.
- Present a slide show.
- Write a book and make an oral report about it.
- Make a tape recording.
- Write a play and perform it for the class.
- Make an oral report with posters and wall charts as visual aids.

The kind of presentation you plan will let you know whether or not you need to look for things like pictures, charts, or quotes as you do your research.

98 **Level C** • Achieve Mastery

Plan Your Research

Before you finalize your topic, take a trip to the library to make sure the material you need is really there. Check general reference materials, like encyclopedias, for a brief overview of your topic. Check the card catalog and magazine indexes. Go on the Internet if you can. Consider using resources like these:

- Books, magazines, and newspapers
- People to interview
- An experiment, survey, or observation of your own
- Organizations to write to
- Videos and cassettes
- CD-ROMs or Web sites

Don't overlook interviewing an expert on your topic. Many people will be happy to share their knowledge and experience with you.

Your Project Notebook—Your Most Important Resource

As soon as a project is assigned, start a project notebook or set aside a special section for your project in your school notebook. Your project notebook will improve your organization by giving you a special place to record all the information you find. Begin by writing down possible topics. As you choose and narrow your topic, add important ideas that support your opinion. When you check the library for possible research materials, record the names and locations of sources that look interesting. You can come back to them later, when it's time to begin your research. A project notebook will help you save time and avoid stress. You'll always have all the information you need right at hand.

Here are some sections you might have in your project notebook:

- Topics
- Key Words
- Research Questions
- References and Other Sources
- Experiments and Observations
- Bibliography

Where Are You Going?

Summarize what you learned in this lesson. ____________________

Now use your summary to write a ***Take Charge!*** goal that will help you become a better student.

Unit 8 • Preparing Speeches, Reports, and Projects 99

Collecting and Organizing Information

About Collecting and Organizing

The secret ingredients for effective information-gathering are organization and orderliness. Forming efficient habits now will help students throughout their lives, whether they're writing a research paper or making a decision about buying a car or a television set. In this lesson, students will learn a step-by-step process for researching information about a topic they have chosen and for organizing the information to prepare a presentation.

Pages 100–101

◆ **Information, Please! Where Do You Stand?**
After students read the introduction, remind them that they chose topics in the last lesson. Suggest that they keep a topic that interests them in mind as they answer the *Where Do You Stand?* questions. Invite volunteers to share the answers they wrote. Hold a class discussion about the merits of different research techniques, including any special steps you require students to complete.

◆ **Organize Your Thoughts**
Discuss the sample web. Remind students that they could add subtopics by drawing lines from the smaller circles. Then students can work with a partner who has similar interests to brainstorm ideas about a topic.

◆ **Plan Your Research**
Ask partners to share their lists of sources. If necessary, introduce other ideas, such as letters to museums or university libraries or departments. Be sure students know how to use standard library research tools such as the catalog, computer databases, the *Readers' Guide to Periodical Literature,* and the Dewey decimal system. Also, warn students never to contact or meet with anyone without the consent and presence of parents or teachers. Share some of your own tips for collecting information (see *Teacher Modeling*).

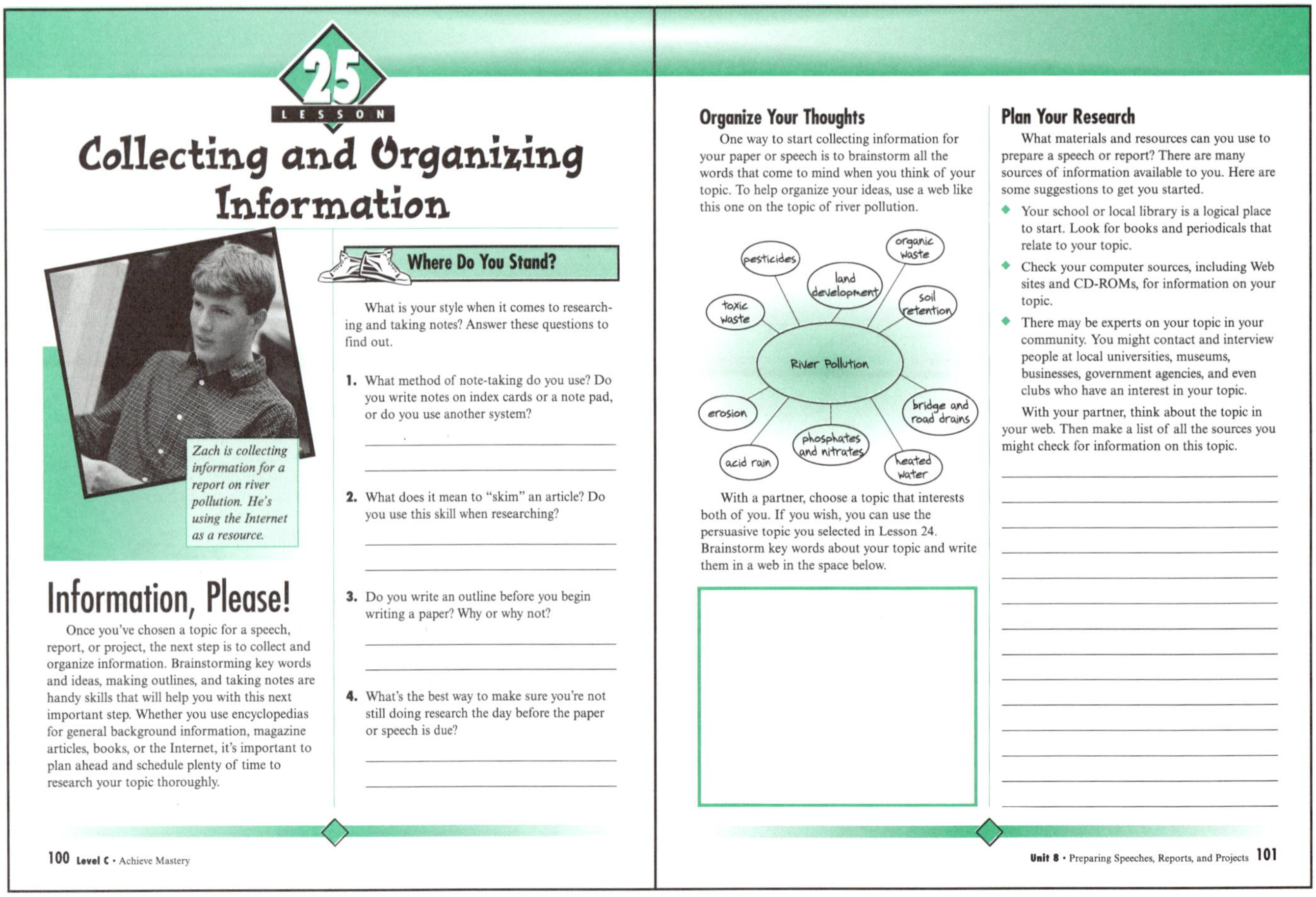

25 LESSON

Collecting and Organizing Information

Zach is collecting information for a report on river pollution. He's using the Internet as a resource.

Information, Please!

Once you've chosen a topic for a speech, report, or project, the next step is to collect and organize information. Brainstorming key words and ideas, making outlines, and taking notes are handy skills that will help you with this next important step. Whether you use encyclopedias for general background information, magazine articles, books, or the Internet, it's important to plan ahead and schedule plenty of time to research your topic thoroughly.

Where Do You Stand?

What is your style when it comes to researching and taking notes? Answer these questions to find out.

1. What method of note-taking do you use? Do you write notes on index cards or a note pad, or do you use another system?
2. What does it mean to "skim" an article? Do you use this skill when researching?
3. Do you write an outline before you begin writing a paper? Why or why not?
4. What's the best way to make sure you're not still doing research the day before the paper or speech is due?

100 Level C • Achieve Mastery

Organize Your Thoughts

One way to start collecting information for your paper or speech is to brainstorm all the words that come to mind when you think of your topic. To help organize your ideas, use a web like this one on the topic of river pollution.

River Pollution
pesticides
land development
organic waste
soil retention
toxic waste
erosion
phosphates and nitrates
bridge and road drains
acid rain
heated water

With a partner, choose a topic that interests both of you. If you wish, you can use the persuasive topic you selected in Lesson 24. Brainstorm key words about your topic and write them in a web in the space below.

Plan Your Research

What materials and resources can you use to prepare a speech or report? There are many sources of information available to you. Here are some suggestions to get you started.

- Your school or local library is a logical place to start. Look for books and periodicals that relate to your topic.
- Check your computer sources, including Web sites and CD-ROMs, for information on your topic.
- There may be experts on your topic in your community. You might contact and interview people at local universities, museums, businesses, government agencies, and even clubs who have an interest in your topic.

With your partner, think about the topic in your web. Then make a list of all the sources you might check for information on this topic.

Unit 8 • Preparing Speeches, Reports, and Projects 101

Pages 102–103

- **Tips for Collecting and Organizing Information**
  Students can read the tips for a step-by-step guide to collecting and organizing research information. Ask students to practice skimming and scanning textbooks or other sources. As you discuss tip 4, *Take Notes,* remind students that words are not the only recording option. They may also want to make charts and diagrams or note pictures they plan to show. Allow time for students to practice writing bibliography entries. Remind students of the K-W-L chart on page 83. Explain that they can use the chart for research by adding an *H: How will I find out what I want to know?*
- **Where Are You Going?**
  Ask students to write a goal for collecting and organizing information.

Teacher Modeling

You may wish to use or adapt these examples of teacher modeling.

I still use information collecting and organizing techniques when:

- I write a paper for a graduate school class.
- I make a presentation to groups of parents or colleagues or to organizations I belong to.
- I need to make a buying decision.

To collect and organize information:

- I begin by making a project notebook.
- I keep a list of terms to look up and questions to answer.
- I make a list of sources to consult.
- I write facts on cards to organize and reorganize.
- I record my findings in an outline, a web, or an organizer like a pros and cons chart.

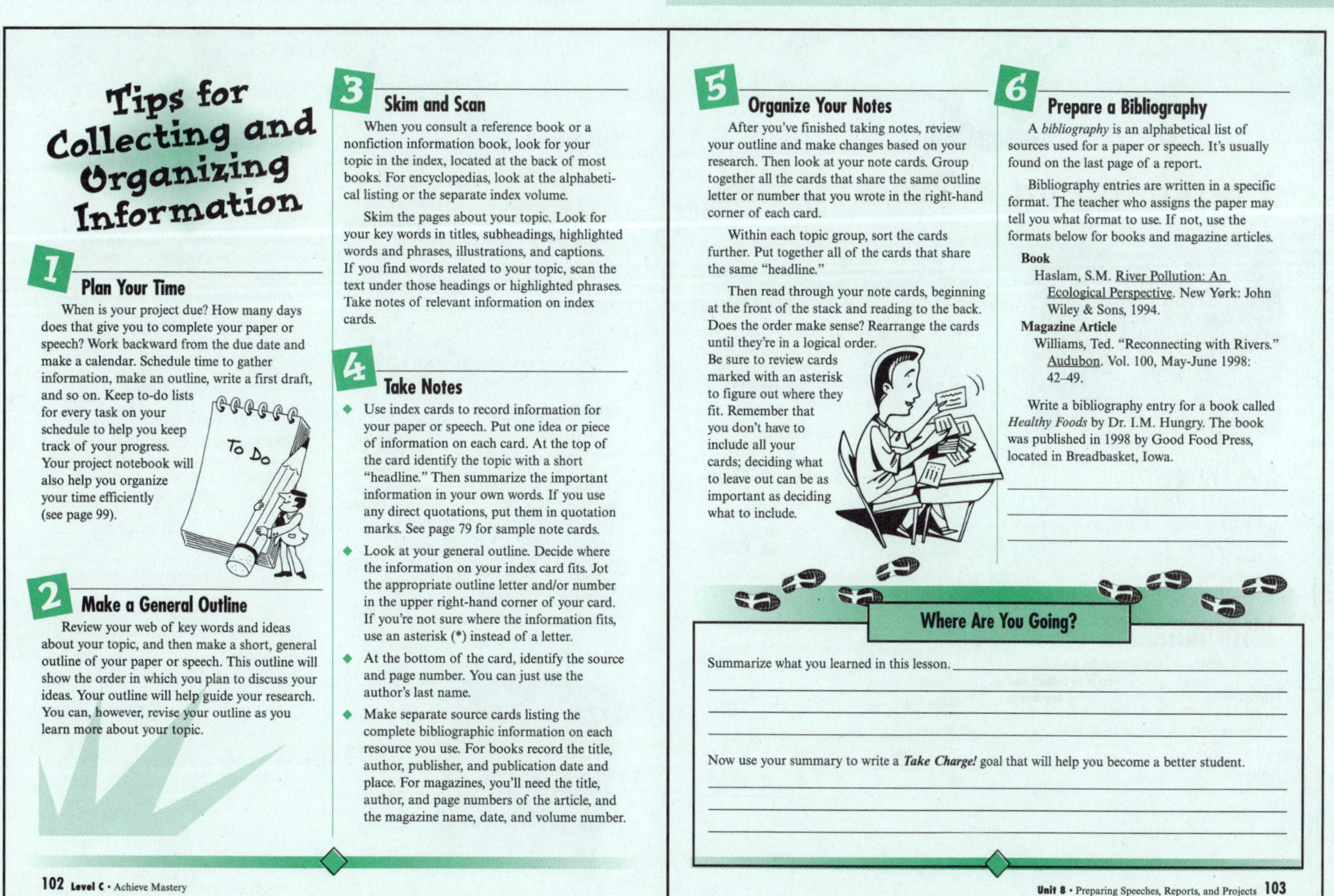

Tips for Collecting and Organizing Information

1 Plan Your Time

When is your project due? How many days does that give you to complete your paper or speech? Work backward from the due date and make a calendar. Schedule time to gather information, make an outline, write a first draft, and so on. Keep to-do lists for every task on your schedule to help you keep track of your progress. Your project notebook will also help you organize your time efficiently (see page 99).

2 Make a General Outline

Review your web of key words and ideas about your topic, and then make a short, general outline of your paper or speech. This outline will show the order in which you plan to discuss your ideas. Your outline will help guide your research. You can, however, revise your outline as you learn more about your topic.

3 Skim and Scan

When you consult a reference book or a nonfiction information book, look for your topic in the index, located at the back of most books. For encyclopedias, look at the alphabetical listing or the separate index volume.

Skim the pages about your topic. Look for your key words in titles, subheadings, highlighted words and phrases, illustrations, and captions. If you find words related to your topic, scan the text under those headings or highlighted phrases. Take notes of relevant information on index cards.

4 Take Notes

- Use index cards to record information for your paper or speech. Put one idea or piece of information on each card. At the top of the card identify the topic with a short "headline." Then summarize the important information in your own words. If you use any direct quotations, put them in quotation marks. See page 79 for sample note cards.
- Look at your general outline. Decide where the information on your index card fits. Jot the appropriate outline letter and/or number in the upper right-hand corner of your card. If you're not sure where the information fits, use an asterisk (*) instead of a letter.
- At the bottom of the card, identify the source and page number. You can just use the author's last name.
- Make separate source cards listing the complete bibliographic information on each resource you use. For books record the title, author, publisher, and publication date and place. For magazines, you'll need the title, author, and page numbers of the article, and the magazine name, date, and volume number.

102 Level C • Achieve Mastery

5 Organize Your Notes

After you've finished taking notes, review your outline and make changes based on your research. Then look at your note cards. Group together all the cards that share the same outline letter or number that you wrote in the right-hand corner of each card.

Within each topic group, sort the cards further. Put together all of the cards that share the same "headline."

Then read through your note cards, beginning at the front of the stack and reading to the back. Does the order make sense? Rearrange the cards until they're in a logical order. Be sure to review cards marked with an asterisk to figure out where they fit. Remember that you don't have to include all your cards; deciding what to leave out can be as important as deciding what to include.

6 Prepare a Bibliography

A *bibliography* is an alphabetical list of sources used for a paper or speech. It's usually found on the last page of a report.

Bibliography entries are written in a specific format. The teacher who assigns the paper may tell you what format to use. If not, use the formats below for books and magazine articles.

Book

Haslam, S.M. River Pollution: An Ecological Perspective. New York: John Wiley & Sons, 1994.

Magazine Article

Williams, Ted. "Reconnecting with Rivers." Audubon. Vol. 100, May-June 1998: 42–49.

Write a bibliography entry for a book called *Healthy Foods* by Dr. I.M. Hungry. The book was published in 1998 by Good Food Press, located in Breadbasket, Iowa.

______

Where Are You Going?

Summarize what you learned in this lesson. ______

Now use your summary to write a *Take Charge!* goal that will help you become a better student.

______

Unit 8 • Preparing Speeches, Reports, and Projects 103

26 LESSON Preparing for a Presentation

About Presentations

Even one of the world's greatest actors, Sir Laurence Olivier, suffered from debilitating stage fright. For many adolescents, the fear can be even worse. Step-by-step practical techniques for preparing and making presentations can help students overcome their fears through the only effective method for combating stage fright: experience. In this lesson, students will learn sure-fire strategies for successful presentations. This will enable students to build the confidence they need to overcome their fears.

Pages 104–105

◆ **The Three Ps**
Read the introduction with your students. Ask volunteers to share experiences of stage fright and tell about times they have used any of the steps in *The Three Ps*.

◆ **Where Do You Stand?/Rate Yourself**
Ask students to complete the quiz to evaluate their current presentation techniques. Help students see the relationship between successful preparation and presentation techniques and the feeling of confidence that keeps stage fright away. During a class discussion about how each technique improves a speech, share some of your own tips for making successful presentations (see *Teacher Modeling*).

◆ **What Do You Mean?**
Students will enjoy using tone of voice to change the meaning of a simple sentence. They'll also learn that delivery can make a big difference.

◆ **Evaluate the Speaker**
If possible, provide a videotape of a famous speech or show a presentation taped from TV. In a follow-up discussion, invite students to compare their answers to the questions and tell what they learned about what to do and what *not* to do while presenting a speech.

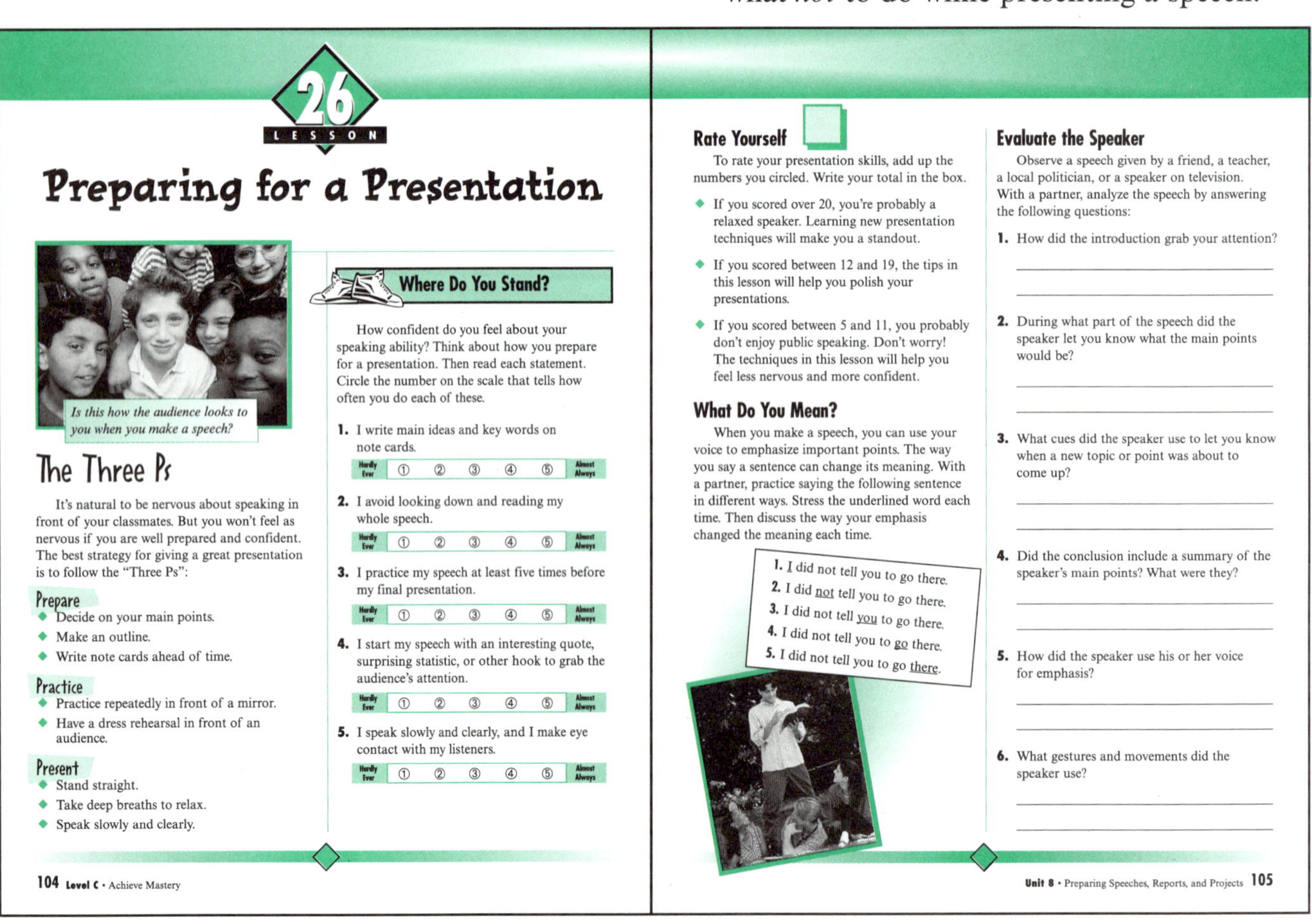

26 LESSON

Preparing for a Presentation

Is this how the audience looks to you when you make a speech?

The Three Ps

It's natural to be nervous about speaking in front of your classmates. But you won't feel as nervous if you are well prepared and confident. The best strategy for giving a great presentation is to follow the "Three Ps":

Prepare
- Decide on your main points.
- Make an outline.
- Write note cards ahead of time.

Practice
- Practice repeatedly in front of a mirror.
- Have a dress rehearsal in front of an audience.

Present
- Stand straight.
- Take deep breaths to relax.
- Speak slowly and clearly.

Where Do You Stand?

How confident do you feel about your speaking ability? Think about how you prepare for a presentation. Then read each statement. Circle the number on the scale that tells how often you do each of these.

1. I write main ideas and key words on note cards.
   Hardly Ever ① ② ③ ④ ⑤ Almost Always
2. I avoid looking down and reading my whole speech.
   Hardly Ever ① ② ③ ④ ⑤ Almost Always
3. I practice my speech at least five times before my final presentation.
   Hardly Ever ① ② ③ ④ ⑤ Almost Always
4. I start my speech with an interesting quote, surprising statistic, or other hook to grab the audience's attention.
   Hardly Ever ① ② ③ ④ ⑤ Almost Always
5. I speak slowly and clearly, and I make eye contact with my listeners.
   Hardly Ever ① ② ③ ④ ⑤ Almost Always

104 Level C • Achieve Mastery

Rate Yourself

To rate your presentation skills, add up the numbers you circled. Write your total in the box.

- If you scored over 20, you're probably a relaxed speaker. Learning new presentation techniques will make you a standout.
- If you scored between 12 and 19, the tips in this lesson will help you polish your presentations.
- If you scored between 5 and 11, you probably don't enjoy public speaking. Don't worry! The techniques in this lesson will help you feel less nervous and more confident.

What Do You Mean?

When you make a speech, you can use your voice to emphasize important points. The way you say a sentence can change its meaning. With a partner, practice saying the following sentence in different ways. Stress the underlined word each time. Then discuss the way your emphasis changed the meaning each time.

1. I did not tell you to go there.
2. I did not tell you to go there.
3. I did not tell you to go there.
4. I did not tell you to go there.
5. I did not tell you to go there.

Evaluate the Speaker

Observe a speech given by a friend, a teacher, a local politician, or a speaker on television. With a partner, analyze the speech by answering the following questions:

1. How did the introduction grab your attention?
2. During what part of the speech did the speaker let you know what the main points would be?
3. What cues did the speaker use to let you know when a new topic or point was about to come up?
4. Did the conclusion include a summary of the speaker's main points? What were they?
5. How did the speaker use his or her voice for emphasis?
6. What gestures and movements did the speaker use?

Unit 8 • Preparing Speeches, Reports, and Projects 105

Pages 106–107

- **Remember the Three Ps!**
These tips expand on the ideas in the lesson introduction. They'll also help students recognize that the key to making successful speeches and presentations is to break the large task into small, manageable steps. Ask a volunteer to read each section aloud. Make sure students notice that the *Present* tips can be adapted to make a general outline for any oral or written presentation.
- **Speech-Making Tips**
After students read the tips, invite them to add tips they've learned on their own from making speeches and evaluating speeches presented by others.
- **Where Are You Going?**
Ask students to write a goal that will help them improve their oral presentation techniques.

Teacher Modeling

You may wish to use or adapt these examples of teacher modeling.

To make a presentation interesting to my audience:

- I think about what they already know about my topic.
- I decide what they might need to know in order to understand my main ideas.
- I try to anticipate questions audience members might ask.

To attract and hold the attention of my audience:

- I tell anecdotes to illustrate important points instead of just stating dry facts.
- I start with an unexpected quotation or a shocking statistic.
- I may tell a joke if it is appropriate and I think I can tell it effectively.

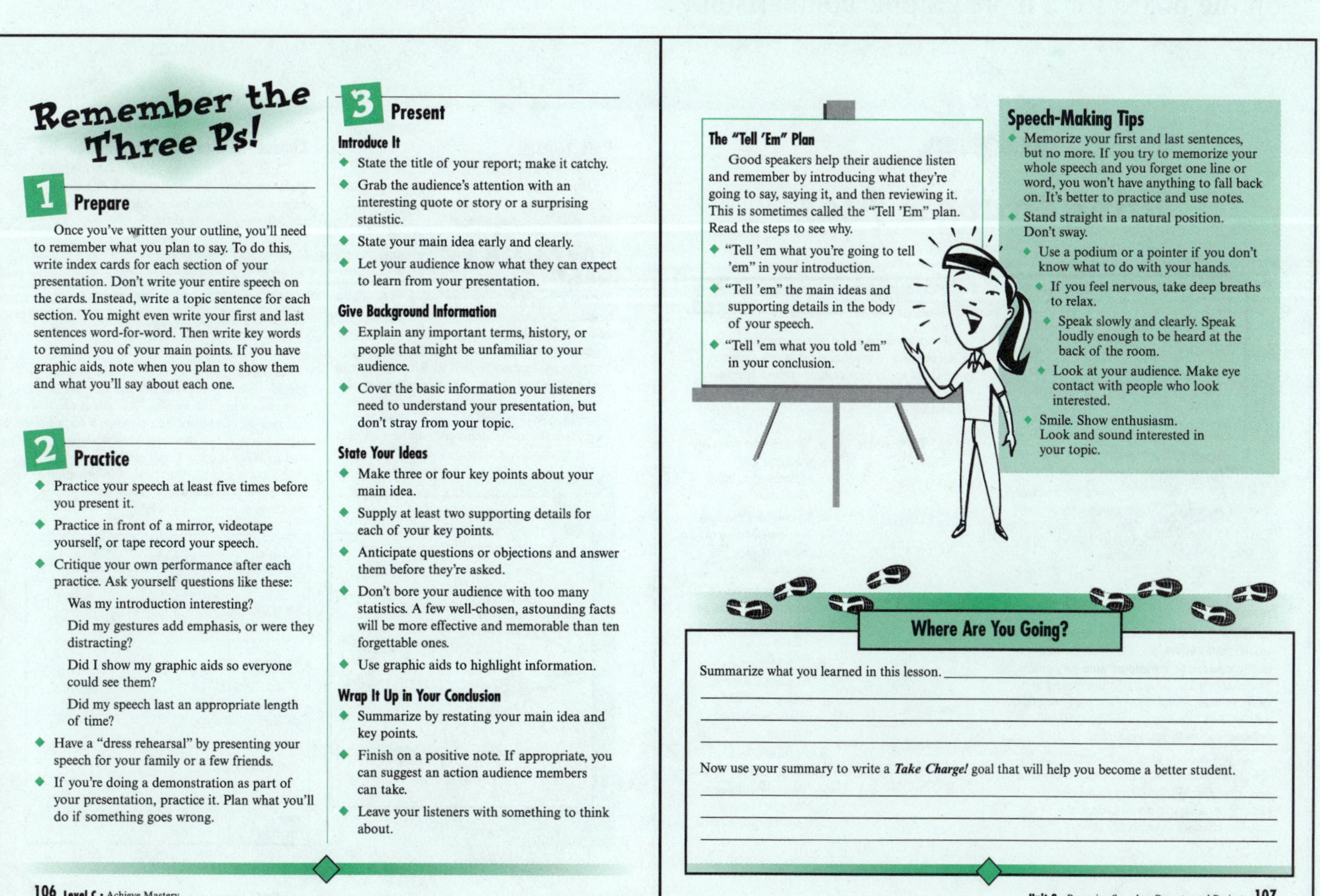

Remember the Three Ps!

1 Prepare

Once you've written your outline, you'll need to remember what you plan to say. To do this, write index cards for each section of your presentation. Don't write your entire speech on the cards. Instead, write a topic sentence for each section. You might even write your first and last sentences word-for-word. Then write key words to remind you of your main points. If you have graphic aids, note when you plan to show them and what you'll say about each one.

2 Practice

- Practice your speech at least five times before you present it.
- Practice in front of a mirror, videotape yourself, or tape record your speech.
- Critique your own performance after each practice. Ask yourself questions like these:
  - Was my introduction interesting?
  - Did my gestures add emphasis, or were they distracting?
  - Did I show my graphic aids so everyone could see them?
  - Did my speech last an appropriate length of time?
- Have a "dress rehearsal" by presenting your speech for your family or a few friends.
- If you're doing a demonstration as part of your presentation, practice it. Plan what you'll do if something goes wrong.

3 Present

Introduce It

- State the title of your report; make it catchy.
- Grab the audience's attention with an interesting quote or story or a surprising statistic.
- State your main idea early and clearly.
- Let your audience know what they can expect to learn from your presentation.

Give Background Information

- Explain any important terms, history, or people that might be unfamiliar to your audience.
- Cover the basic information your listeners need to understand your presentation, but don't stray from your topic.

State Your Ideas

- Make three or four key points about your main idea.
- Supply at least two supporting details for each of your key points.
- Anticipate questions or objections and answer them before they're asked.
- Don't bore your audience with too many statistics. A few well-chosen, astounding facts will be more effective and memorable than ten forgettable ones.
- Use graphic aids to highlight information.

Wrap It Up in Your Conclusion

- Summarize by restating your main idea and key points.
- Finish on a positive note. If appropriate, you can suggest an action audience members can take.
- Leave your listeners with something to think about.

106 Level C • Achieve Mastery

The "Tell 'Em" Plan

Good speakers help their audience listen and remember by introducing what they're going to say, saying it, and then reviewing it. This is sometimes called the "Tell 'Em" plan. Read the steps to see why.

- "Tell 'em what you're going to tell 'em" in your introduction.
- "Tell 'em" the main ideas and supporting details in the body of your speech.
- "Tell 'em what you told 'em" in your conclusion.

Speech-Making Tips

- Memorize your first and last sentences, but no more. If you try to memorize your whole speech and you forget one line or word, you won't have anything to fall back on. It's better to practice and use notes.
- Stand straight in a natural position. Don't sway.
- Use a podium or a pointer if you don't know what to do with your hands.
- If you feel nervous, take deep breaths to relax.
- Speak slowly and clearly. Speak loudly enough to be heard at the back of the room.
- Look at your audience. Make eye contact with people who look interested.
- Smile. Show enthusiasm. Look and sound interested in your topic.

Where Are You Going?

Summarize what you learned in this lesson. ____________

Now use your summary to write a *Take Charge!* goal that will help you become a better student.

Unit 8 • Preparing Speeches, Reports, and Projects 107

Using Graphic Aids

About Graphic Aids

Graphic aids such as pictures and charts help speakers make important points and make a presentation more interesting for the audience. This is especially true for today's students who have become accustomed to learning visually as they watch television and use computers. But some students may be reluctant to go to the extra trouble of preparing graphic aids. In this lesson, students will learn good reasons for using graphic aids in reports and presentations. They'll also learn about different kinds of graphic aids and the most appropriate times to use each one.

Pages 108–109

◆ **A Gem of an Idea**
Invite a volunteer to read the introduction. Then have a student put the information from the chart into words. If time allows, you may even want to record the student's explanation on the board for a more graphic comparison. Afterward, students should have no trouble answering the question in the caption.

◆ **Where Do You Stand?/Rate Yourself**
Use the quiz results to evaluate whether or not your students are familiar with different kinds of graphic aids. If necessary, display examples of different kinds of visuals.

◆ **Is One Picture Worth a Thousand Words?**
Ask students to cover their books before beginning the activity. Ask one person in each pair to give directions and the other to draw. Suggest that pairs time themselves to see how long it took to describe the diagram.

◆ **Choose the Most Effective Graphic Aid**
This activity makes the point that different graphic aids serve different purposes. Successful graphic aids are tailored to their presentations. After students complete the chart and discuss their ideas, share some of your own ideas about choosing and using graphic aids (see *Teacher Modeling*).

27
LESSON

Using Graphic Aids

Gem Name	Mineral	Usual Colors
Amethyst	quartz	purple
Diamond	carbon	bluish white
Emerald	beryl	green
Opal	opal	red, green, blue
Ruby	corundum	red
Sapphire	corundum	blue

Do you think it would be easier to learn this information by listening to it or by seeing it on a chart?

A Gem of an Idea

If you had heard the facts about gems in a speech instead of reading them in a chart, you might have found the information very confusing. The chart makes the information clearer and easier to understand. That's the purpose of all graphic aids—to help you understand and communicate information better.

As you prepare for a presentation, think about its contents. Which of your ideas could you show graphically? Then create and use photographs, charts, graphs, diagrams, or maps to enhance your presentation.

Where Do You Stand?

How familiar are you with the purposes of different types of graphic aids? Match each graphic aid in the first column with its purpose in the second column. Write the matching letter in the blank.

1. ___ Photograph
2. ___ Diagram
3. ___ Chart or table
4. ___ Map
5. ___ Graph

a. To show the parts or workings of something, usually with labels
b. To compare changes over time of two or more sets of information
c. To present a set of facts in an organized way, often in labeled columns
d. To help listeners visualize a setting, people, or other details mentioned in a speech
e. To show where things such as political boundaries, roads, or natural resources are located

108 Level C • Achieve Mastery

Rate Yourself

ANSWERS: 1. d, 2. a, 3. c, 4. e, 5. b.

How accurately did you identify the purposes of different types of graphic aids? Congratulations if you matched all five!

Is One Picture Worth a Thousand Words?

Sometimes a diagram can convey information better than words alone. Study the diagram below. Then ask a partner to draw a similar diagram by following your verbal instructions. Tell your partner not to look at this page until he or she is finished. Talk your partner through the drawing and try to help him or her "see" your description well enough to draw it. When the diagram is finished, discuss the number of words it took to describe a simple picture.

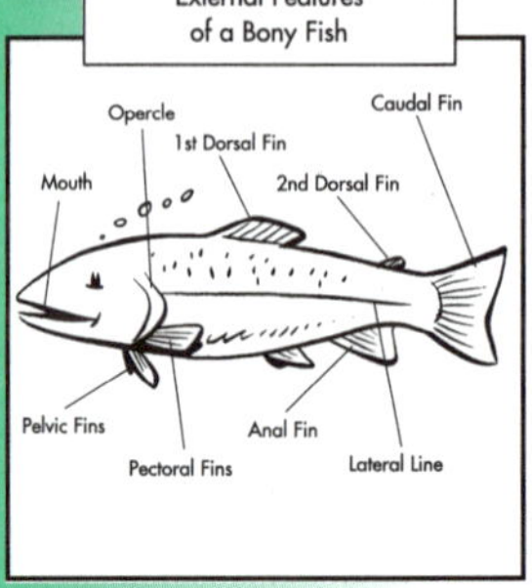

External Features of a Bony Fish

Opercle
1st Dorsal Fin
Caudal Fin
Mouth
2nd Dorsal Fin
Pelvic Fins
Anal Fin
Pectoral Fins
Lateral Line

Choose the Most Effective Graphic Aid

Look for examples of graphic aids in your social studies textbook, magazines, or newspapers. Find at least one example of each of the following graphic aids:

- ☐ bar graph
- ☐ line graph
- ☐ circle graph or pie chart
- ☐ chart or table
- ☐ map

In a small group, analyze and compare the graphic aids. Discuss how effective they are in communicating information. Talk about why one type of graphic aid accompanies a certain type of article. For example, when is a map useful? When is a bar graph more appropriate than a circle graph? What type of information does a chart or table convey best? Write your conclusions in the chart below.

Graphic Aid:	Most Useful for:
bar graph	
line graph	
circle graph or pie chart	
chart or table	
map	

Unit 8 • Preparing Speeches, Reports, and Projects 109

Pages 110–111

- **Seven Useful Graphic Aids**
  Ask volunteers to read about the purposes of diagrams, photographs, maps, charts and tables, and bar, line, and circle graphs. Encourage students to name specific presentation topics each graphic aid could enhance effectively.
- **Helpful Hints for Graphic Aids**
  Ask students to read these tips for putting graphic aids to work in their presentations. Invite volunteers to add their own tips.
- **Wise Words**
  By expanding on the proverb and putting the idea into their own words, students will summarize the main points of this lesson.
- **Where Are You Going?**
  Ask students to write a goal that will help them enhance their presentations with graphic aids.

Teacher Modeling

You may wish to use or adapt these examples of teacher modeling.

To decide how I can use graphic aids most effectively:

- I look for ideas that may be difficult for my audience to understand without extra help.
- I look for ideas I want to emphasize.

To decide what kind of graphic aid to use:

- I look through my notes to find charts and pictures.
- I sketch the graphic aid to make sure it really says what I intend it to say.

When I use a graphic aid:

- I make sure everyone in the audience can see it.
- I write notes on the back so I won't have to turn the graphic aid away from the audience to look at it as I speak.

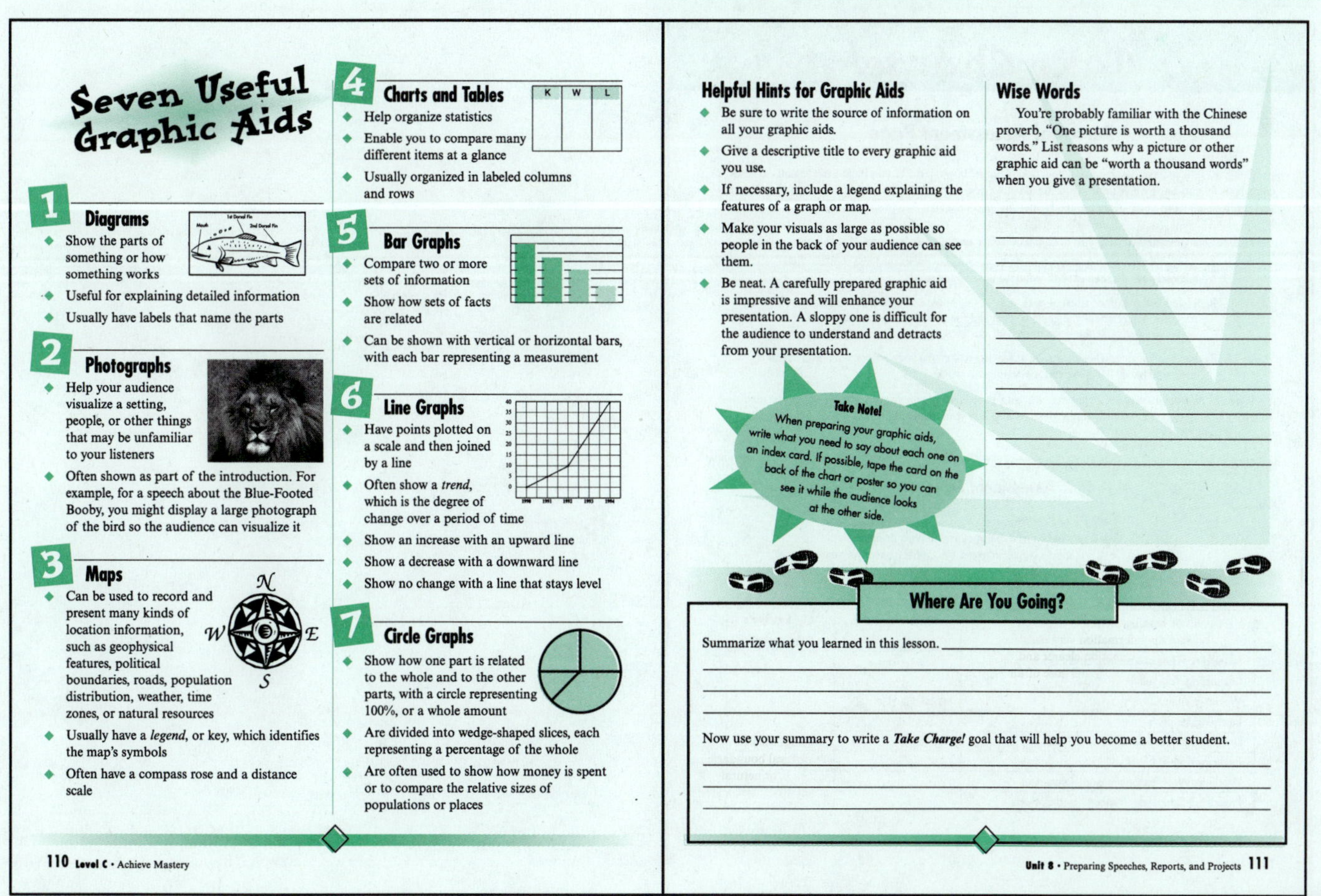

Seven Useful Graphic Aids

1 Diagrams
- Show the parts of something or how something works
- Useful for explaining detailed information
- Usually have labels that name the parts

2 Photographs
- Help your audience visualize a setting, people, or other things that may be unfamiliar to your listeners
- Often shown as part of the introduction. For example, for a speech about the Blue-Footed Booby, you might display a large photograph of the bird so the audience can visualize it

3 Maps
- Can be used to record and present many kinds of location information, such as geophysical features, political boundaries, roads, population distribution, weather, time zones, or natural resources
- Usually have a *legend*, or key, which identifies the map's symbols
- Often have a compass rose and a distance scale

4 Charts and Tables
- Help organize statistics
- Enable you to compare many different items at a glance
- Usually organized in labeled columns and rows

5 Bar Graphs
- Compare two or more sets of information
- Show how sets of facts are related
- Can be shown with vertical or horizontal bars, with each bar representing a measurement

6 Line Graphs
- Have points plotted on a scale and then joined by a line
- Often show a *trend*, which is the degree of change over a period of time
- Show an increase with an upward line
- Show a decrease with a downward line
- Show no change with a line that stays level

7 Circle Graphs
- Show how one part is related to the whole and to the other parts, with a circle representing 100%, or a whole amount
- Are divided into wedge-shaped slices, each representing a percentage of the whole
- Are often used to show how money is spent or to compare the relative sizes of populations or places

110 Level C • Achieve Mastery

Helpful Hints for Graphic Aids
- Be sure to write the source of information on all your graphic aids.
- Give a descriptive title to every graphic aid you use.
- If necessary, include a legend explaining the features of a graph or map.
- Make your visuals as large as possible so people in the back of your audience can see them.
- Be neat. A carefully prepared graphic aid is impressive and will enhance your presentation. A sloppy one is difficult for the audience to understand and detracts from your presentation.

Take Note!
When preparing your graphic aids, write what you need to say about each one on an index card. If possible, tape the card on the back of the chart or poster so you can see it while the audience looks at the other side.

Wise Words
You're probably familiar with the Chinese proverb, "One picture is worth a thousand words." List reasons why a picture or other graphic aid can be "worth a thousand words" when you give a presentation.

Where Are You Going?
Summarize what you learned in this lesson. ____

Now use your summary to write a *Take Charge!* goal that will help you become a better student.

Unit 8 • Preparing Speeches, Reports, and Projects 111

Page 112

Personal Assessment

The assessment page invites students to reflect on their progress and helps them take responsibility for making ongoing improvements to their study skills. The completed page may contribute to a formal grade, or may simply provide an opportunity for self-reflection and conferencing.

Ask a volunteer to read the three-part directions aloud. Allow time for students to review the goals they wrote at the end of each lesson. Encourage students to think about specific evidence they might give to show that they have achieved a goal. Invite volunteers to read goals they wrote and describe actions they have taken to achieve them.

Point out the unit titles in the assessment chart and explain that they name important categories of study skills. Encourage students to think about each area as a whole as they complete their self-assessment.

Use the assessment scale to add your own ratings to each student's page. Take the opportunity to hold individual conferences to talk about the completed assessments. Discuss similarities and differences between students' ratings and your own. Celebrate students' accomplishments and help them plan ways to continue improving their skills.

You Can **Take Charge!**

Personal Assessment Page

Congratulations! You've finished your ***Take Charge!*** book. You've completed the lessons and set goals to help you improve your study skills. By now, you've probably been able to make some changes and improvements in your study habits. Hopefully, you've seen some positive results!

This page is designed to help you and your teacher assess your progress. Here's how it works:

1. At the end of every lesson, you summarized what you learned and wrote a ***Take Charge!*** goal. Reread each of your summaries and goals.
2. Listed below are the titles of each unit of this book and a scale for assessing your progress. Think about the goals you set and the progress you have made. Then, assess yourself. Use the scale to record your progress.
3. Next, it's your teacher's turn. Your teacher will assess your progress using the same scale and his or her observations about your work.

When both assessments are complete, you and your teacher can compare and discuss the results. Together, you may come up with some ideas to improve your study skills even more. Like the title of this book says, *You Can Take Charge!*

Assessment Scale

1 = I do well in this area.
2 = I've made some changes and shown improvement.
3 = I've made some progress, but I still have a long way to go.
4 = I haven't worked on this. I'd better get started!

	My Assessment	My Teacher's Assessment
Managing Time, Materials, and Space		
Managing Yourself		
Working With Others		
Studying for Tests		
Developing Test-Taking Skills		
Participating in Class		
Working With Textbooks and References		
Preparing Speeches, Reports, and Projects		

112